NOTHING SACRED

N✡THING SACRED

The Truth About Judaism

DOUGLAS RUSHKOFF

 THREE RIVERS PRESS • NEW YORK

Published by Three Rivers Press, New York, New York.
Member of the Crown Publishing Group, a division of Random House, Inc.
www.crownpublishing.com

THREE RIVERS PRESS and the Tugboat design are registered trademarks
of Random House, Inc.

Originally published in slightly different form in hardcover by
Crown Publishers, a division of Random House, Inc., in 2003.

Printed in the United States of America

DESIGN BY BARBARA STURMAN

Library of Congress Cataloging-in-Publication Data
Rushkoff, Douglas.
    Nothing sacred : the truth about Judaism / Douglas Rushkoff.
        p. cm.
    Includes bibliographical references and index.
    1. Judaism—Essence, genius, nature. I. Title.
BM565 .R87 2003
296.3—dc21   2002031188

ISBN 1-4000-5139-8

10 9 8 7 6 5 4 3 2 1

First Paperback Edition

For my wife, Barbara

CONTENTS

PREFACE

WHAT I'VE TRIED TO DO with this book is find and share the best arguments in Judaism for its own evolution—even if this evolution looks to some like Judaism's very dissolution. For many of the things happening in a vast majority of synagogues and philanthropies today have little to do with Jewishness. To me, anyway, they represent some of the same institutional, ethnocentric, and nationalist tendencies that Judaism was invented to dispel.

In order to grasp the sense of this admittedly critical stance—one shared by about half of America's Jews, in fact—we must come to understand Judaism as an ongoing process rather than a list of rules and beliefs set in stone. Jewish continuity is not the maintenance of rituals and behaviors from a particular moment in history, but the continuing journey away from the mind-sets that lead to unkind, unholy lives. It is this challenge that remains the same, which is why its expression must constantly evolve.

Ancient Israelites may have had trouble breaking their emotional attachment to the comforting animal gods of Egypt or, later, giving up the sacrifices of animals at the Holy Temple.

If today's Jews are truly concerned about continuity, then they can't content themselves with the profound achievements of two or three thousand years ago. They must look instead toward the beliefs and ideas that stunt holiness today. However challenging or even painful, Jews must evaluate the comforting but ultimately destructive contention that God loves his Jews the best, or that he has set aside a particular nation for them. This doesn't mean abandoning Judaism or Israel, but rather examining the religious fundamentalism used to justify them.

Because to me, Judaism has always seemed less like a religion than the process by which we *get over* religion. It was intended as a path not to complacency or self-satisfaction, but to questions and action.

We can choose to live up to the beliefs and practices of our ancestors in one of two ways. The first is to imitate them exactly, as best we can. This will preserve their formulaic accuracy, but freeze our faith in history. Our ethics, ideas, and social awareness will be the same as they were two thousand years ago. The alternative is to discern the intent of our ancestors' codes of law and then figure out today's equivalents. This requires work, thought, collaboration, and a commitment to spiritual growth. Not an easy sell, these days, when times seem so hard. The world appears committed to a new round of holy wars, the Middle East is as far from a lasting peace as ever it was, anti-Semitism is on the rise in Europe, and even those of us in the West are no longer impervious to the threat of terrorism.

It's no wonder many people are rushing back to their religions, including Judaism, for reassurance—for a way of fitting the world's ongoing chaos into a bigger story. To reconstruct the narratives that are being shattered.

But, as I hope to show, religions aren't necessarily functioning at their best when they provide pat answers to life's biggest questions. Judaism, in particular, favors open-ended inquiry over unilateral decree. Given our global predicament, the challenge to Jews and to all thinking people is to resist the temptation to fall into a polarized, nationalist, or, God forbid, self-righteously holy posture.

I've spent most of my professional life studying and writing about new media, and if the interactive age has taught me anything it is that narratives serve our best interests only when we take responsibility for authoring them. We are all writing the future of history, together.

Likewise, as Jews, rather than retreating into the simplistic and childlike, if temporarily reassuring, belief that the answers have already been written along with the entire human story, we must resolve to participate actively in writing the story ourselves—the story of our civilization as well as the story of our religion. Endlessly repeating the Judaism of the past turns it into a bedtime tale. It was intended and must serve, instead, as a wake-up call. Indeed, now as much as ever, it's time to grow up and take charge of our collective destiny.

I understand that it's tough to make this leap, particularly for those who have used religion as a retreat or safe haven. It is a frightening moment for a child to realize that his parents are not gods. Likewise, it is frightening for a people to realize that their gods are not parents. We, God help us, are the adults here.

Whether or not our own institutions are up to the challenge, our religions do hold certain keys for developing the kind of autonomy and fortitude that is now required of us. For its part, Judaism's emphasis on iconoclasm, abstract monotheism, and social justice makes it a potentially valuable resource to a world on the brink of adopting their opposites. Although Judaism's outward, obvious manifestation today in temples, religious schools, and Israeli politics often appears anything but thoughtful or pluralistic, its practices and literature still contain the seeds of an extraordinarily progressive and intellectual process that strikes out at blind faith and the fundamentalist passivity it produces.

The experiences gained and insights gleaned after three thousand years of spiritual and ethical debating can offer anyone clear alternatives to the overly concretized narratives that are failing the world—even if we have to move beyond what is currently passing for Judaism in order to find and propagate them.

It's time we wake up from the stories we've been telling ourselves and invent a new one.

NOTHING SACRED

Can we talk?

—JOAN RIVERS

One

THE

TRANSPARENT FAITH

CAN WE TALK? Why am I not surprised that none other than Joan Rivers is responsible for one of the most accurate condensations of the core values of a three-thousand-year-old tradition? Can we talk? Is our subject really up for discussion?

Sadly, for many Jews today, religion is a closed book. Most Jewish institutions offer little more than the calcified shell that once protected the spiritual insights at its core. Disaffected with their synagogues' emphasis on self-preservation and obsession with intermarriage, most Jews looking for an intelligent inquiry into the nature of spirituality have turned elsewhere, or nowhere.

Meanwhile, faced with the chaos of modern life, others have returned to Judaism in the hope of finding a traditional community with concrete values and well-defined rules. These "returnees" run back to Judaism with a blind and desperate faith and are quickly absorbed by "outreach" organizations, which—in return for money—offer compelling evidence that God exists, that the Jews are indeed the Lord's "chosen people," and that those who adhere to this righteous path will never have to ask themselves another difficult question again.

Ironically, the texts and practices making up Judaism were designed to avert just such a scenario. The Jewish tradition stresses transparency, open-ended inquiry, assimilation of the foreign, and a commitment to conscious living. Most of all, it invites inquiry and change. It is a tradition born out of revolution, committed to evolution, and always willing to undergo renaissance at a moment's notice.

Judaism is open to discussion. It can be questioned and reinterpreted; indeed, it is *supposed* to be questioned, continually. This very discussion—this quest to discover the truth about Judaism and then reinterpret it for a new era—is nothing new. It is, rather, a continuation of the Jewish tradition for collaborative reinvention.

While Judaism holds no exclusive claim to iconoclasm, community ethos, or media literacy, its foundation in these values and its ability to translate them into life practices make it an indispensable resource to a civilization experiencing such a series of disorienting shifts. By reviving this tradition's core values within a modern context, and restoring its emphasis on inquiry over certainty and fluidity over sanctity, we may discover a truly rewarding path for disaffected Jews and a set of powerful tools for anyone wrestling with the challenges of contemporary life.

To do so, however, will require that we question our own most sacred assumptions. We must crack the code, penetrate the myths, squash the superstitions, and retire the beliefs that have mired Judaism in protectionism and paranoia. We must shatter the walls surrounding this religion in order to rediscover the core beliefs those walls were meant to protect.

What disturbs me is that an ethical system founded in revolution, modernity, and universally applicable ideas has become so very mired in their opposites. Judaism was a breakthrough concept. By focusing on the ongoing revision of its particular implementations, it positioned itself to remain relevant through millennia of cultural, political, and technological change. Yet now, just as humanity finds itself on the brink of a dramatic shift, Judaism has contracted and retreated, rendering itself one of the last places Jews, or anyone, would turn for guidance and support.

Our civilization is facing the tremendous spiritual, economic, and cultural challenges posed by globalization, the triumph of science over nature, and the incalculable potential of new technologies. Judaism, instead of rising to meet these challenges, is obsessing with self-preservation. Instead of contending with, for example, the impact of market culture on our children, Jewish outreach groups are hiring trend watchers to help them market Judaism to younger audiences. Instead of analyzing and tempering the massive power of global corporations and their commercial expressions on the human psyche, Jewish institutions are reorganizing themselves to function more like them.

At their most daring, Jewish philanthropies fund the highly superficial expressions of "Jewish chic" emerging in today's pop culture. But neither Madonna's fleeting fascination with kabbalah nor a resurgence of klezmer music on New York's Lower East Side demonstrates any more than Judaism's ability to cater to the media's never-ending quest for commodifiable authenticity. Feel-good retreats and countless workshops offering speciously concocted Jewish mysticism do not revitalize the religion; they merely market and trivialize it.

Neither should Judaism be closeted, for the enjoyment of just a few. It is not only our tradition, but our explicit obligation to act as stewards for the greater society. With varying success, Jews such as Freud, Marx, and Einstein have wrestled with the biggest questions of their ages—and their greatest works were fundamentally informed by their Jewish outlooks. Today, those who work in analogous realms are derided as "secular" at best, and more often "lapsed" or, in a recently coined term, "latent" Jews.

I find myself not inspired, but actually embarrassed that my own work in media and cultural criticism is so firmly rooted in a tradition that I now identify with the most retrograde of behaviors and beliefs. To mention my affinity for Jewish ideas is to risk marginalizing my work and associating myself with a group whose most public expressions are contrary to the tolerance, pluralism, and universal truths I aim to convey.

Sometimes I feel like giving up and accepting the fact that Judaism is simply irrelevant. But then, during a talk or while writing an article, I'll realize that I'm quoting Talmud or reinterpreting a biblical myth in order to support an idea. I don't want to deny myself this greater intellectual and sociological context or the reassurance it affords me.

Every once in a while, however, I wonder if we so-called lapsed Jews might be the true keepers of the flame. Maybe it is not only our right, but our responsibility to legitimize the practices of ourselves and our peers by demonstrating their consistency with core Jewish values. Rather than admit defeat and withdraw from the debate about how Judaism should be carried forth into the twenty-first century, maybe we should engage in this discussion on equal footing. The tradition demands that these views be heard and, at the very least, considered before being dismissed.

A radical reappraisal of Judaism's ability to contribute to modernity is long overdue, and our refusal to do so is sending the best minds and voices of a generation to more accessible and less self-obsessed faiths like Buddhism and Hinduism. Not that these alternatives are lacking their own truths; they are not. Still, the challenges ahead are complex and multifaceted, and we should not deprive ourselves of any culture's wisdom—least of all our own.

This means opening the conversation, as Jews have done so many times before, to the ideas of anyone who comes to the table. If Judaism is to extend its own evolution into a fourth millennium, we must learn to regard its most sacred teachings as open for discussion.

Can we talk? Of course we can. We have over twenty centuries of experience in doing just that.

RELIGION ON THE ROAD

A people of Diaspora, Jews' professional choices, cultural tendencies, and even their theology were defined by the experience and realities of exile. The Jews' unique position as perpetual outsiders led them to adopt and promote a wide range of cosmopolitan and inclusive business strategies and ethical standards.

For example, Jewish exiles were not allowed to own or utilize land in many of the countries where they attempted to settle. These prohibitions made professional farming or fishing out of bounds as a means of generating income. But just because they couldn't own real estate didn't mean they couldn't become brokers. With nothing to call their own, Jews found ways to help the people who did have material assets negotiate their transactions. Their specialties became banking and communications—the world's first truly "virtual" professions.

As the Western world's money changers and financial planners, Jews developed some of the banking systems that are still used today. The only players who lacked a home-field advantage wherever they went, Jews insinuated themselves into other people's business as arbitrators and referees. Unencumbered by the Christian restrictions on usury, Jews were free to serve as moneylenders in an increasingly currency-dependent society. Besides, money, interest, and brokerage were still new concepts in many places and regarded with some suspicion—as were the Jews who worked with it. Jews were middlemen, whose job was to promote fair and open trade among other peoples. The transactions that Jews facilitated had to be kept from appearing mysterious, so that no one would feel cheated. Because everyone needed to understand what was going on, an emphasis on transparency was crucial. The more transparent the transactions, the more willing people would be to trade. Such transparency also depended on a certain amount of knowledge and intelligence. As later Jewish political theorists such as Karl Marx understood, the education of the masses is a prerequisite to a truly just economic scheme. Only people who understand what they are doing can avoid being exploited in their financial transactions.

Jews' passion for open transactions was not limited to finance. They also served as translators and cultural guides, helping people in an increasingly mobile and multicultural Mediterranean society to interact with strangers. Jews were professional intermediaries between societies and their "others." As a result, Jews valued motion and cultural exchange. A fluid society with ever-changing boundaries served them better than a closed or static one in which outsiders and new ideas were feared. Jews' ability to adapt to a variety of cultural situations made them experienced navigators of change and intermingling. And the more things changed, the more Jews were needed.

Jews' later interest in the film, television, and entertainment industries found its roots in these early survival imperatives and cultural goals. In this sense, anti-Semites are not entirely unfounded in their claim that Jews are behind a great media conspiracy. What they don't understand, however, is that the Jewish love for media and entertainment is not part of a plan for global conquest. Rather, it is an extension of the very skills they developed over centuries of serving as cultural mediators.

If there is an agenda underlying Jews' dedication to expanding the role of media in people's lives, it is to promote intellectual perspective and the value of pluralism. Like all good communication, media tends to call sacred values into question. Comedy, for instance, and especially what has become known as *Jewish* comedy, requires an audience to distance itself from its most troublesome concerns and see them in a different, less threatening light. Media, then, at its best, is a form of mass education. But education is threatening to anyone whose power is dependent on fear and ignorance. Not surprisingly, the McCarthy anticommunism hearings focused on media and entertainment professionals more than on actual political agitators and gained significant traction by stoking anti-Semitic sentiments.

Their tenuous status as guests of the many nations in which they settled made Jews excellent futurists. Because they never knew when they might be asked, quite unceremoniously, to pack up and move on, they had to keep their ears to the ground at all times. Losing a sense of the prevailing winds could easily prove catastrophic.

These factors combined to make Jews think in terms of the "big picture." The more interconnected a society, the more likely it was to engage in complex transactions requiring Jews' services. And the more inclusive and tolerant a society, the more likely it was to include the Jews, too.

But many cultures experienced pluralism as a threat to their own national and religious values. Rapid cosmopolitan incursions tend to erode a people's sense of integrity, uniqueness, and superiority over others. Whenever such xenophobia took hold, Jews were the first to be blamed. Fear of persecution and sudden expulsion was a pressing motivation for Jews to look for ways in which everything was connected and to promote these perceptions far and wide. After all, if everything is connected into an intricately linked whole, then this disenfranchised nation of perpetual immigrants must be connected, too.

Jews wanted to advance the idea that they must somehow constitute an irreplaceable node in the web. This is why they habitually reframed situations in their larger contexts, always on the lookout for an explanation of the universe as a single whole. Even Einstein's famous quest for a "unified field theory"—one that could bring space and time together into the same thing—can be understood as an extension of this urge toward wholeness and universal inclusion. Nothing, and no one, is left out. Sometimes consciously and sometimes not, the Jews' many achievements were part of an overarching strategy to make themselves indispensable to others. Assimilation was not a sin; it was survival.

Their religion supported them in this effort and evolved to do so even more. The most central prayer, the *Sh'ma* ("The Lord is one"), amounts to a declaration of the unity of the universe. The Exodus story, as it actually appears in the Torah, is an account of how several distinct tribes unified in common self-interest, under a single, abstract God. Traditionally, each region of the ancient world had its own protecting god. By keeping God unnamable and unknowable, Jews could also keep this deity universal.

The iconoclasm intrinsic to the descendants of Abraham—the legendary idol smasher—combined with their role as resident outsiders, kept the Jews in the position of social commentators. It's a legacy of ironic distance from faulty cultural institutions that stretches two millennia and led to everything from Jewish humor to social and labor activism.

It was their struggle for self-preservation as well as their own set of deeply held humanist values that made Jews both the natural enemies of sacred idols and the promoters of open discussion. Jews prized education and uncensored inquiry for their ability to keep people from falling prey to superstitions and unbridled ethnocentrism. The value of such pluralism was often recognized by the societies in which Jews lived. Third-century Romans, for example, purchased ancillary memberships in Jewish synagogues just so they could take part in intellectual conversations that weren't overshadowed by sacrifices and other parochial rites.

For the Jews, a focus on considered debate over ecstatic ritual was more than a stylistic preference. Superstition, worship of animal gods, and the moblike mentality that often resulted were well-recognized precursors to nationalism and xenophobia. Systems of "natural law" don't generally favor the foreigner, so Jews were at pains to slow any movements in that direction. It was to their advantage to promote critical thinking, inquiry, and consideration. Jews developed the first public school systems, in the first and second centuries of the Common Era, most likely toward this end. But their promotion of critical inquiry also made them the first targets of rising dictators or any group hoping to foment nationalist sentiments.

Judaism's approaches to religious expression and preservation were also born out of its members' perennial exile. Jews were a touring company and developed a uniquely portable and durable set of beliefs, rituals, and practices for their road show. Most of their religious prohibitions were designed to help Jews resist the temptations of the land-based, pagan religions practiced by their hosts. Cultic rites, temple prostitution, and supplication to the earth's natural forces were forbidden. Besides, after the destruction of the Temple and conquest of Israel by the Romans in 70 C.E., the Jews had no holy altar on which to carry out such rituals and no land whose fertility needed to be ensured.

Instead, Jews limited their beliefs and practices to those that could be carried out anywhere, with minimal paraphernalia. Everything of value was to be found in their books and scrolls, which went with them from place to place. The kosher laws, more than serving as health codes or superstitious protection, gave Jews a way to create sacred space around them wherever they traveled. *Halakhah* (Jewish law or code of behavior) brings divinity into one's daily activities. Jews devised prayers for eating, for sleeping, and even for seeing the first bloom of spring. As a result, Judaism became less of something a person believed in than something one *did*. The complex set of behavioral codes, such as the separation of meat from dairy, Shabbat from the work week, and clean from unclean, gave exiled Jews a way to define the boundaries between the sacred and profane, and between themselves and all others, that did not depend on the maintenance of the geographical walls that fell, irreparably, to the Romans at the turn of the millennium. But it also made Jews vulnerable to the isolation and paranoia that has come, in modern times, to work against some of their more universal values.

Still, although the Jews had no nation of their own, their commitment to open systems, iconoclasm, and literacy has enabled them to thrive as long as, or actually longer than, any Western civilization. While many of the Jews' deepest-held beliefs have become obscured by an understandably fearful reaction to persecution, inquisition, and extermination, these ideas are still quite accessible, in all their universal applicability, to anyone who opens the Torah or Talmud. It is high time these core values were exhumed and revived.

THE JEWISH TRINITY:
ICONOCLASM, MONOTHEISM, AND
SOCIAL JUSTICE

Not that long ago, I had lunch with an old friend from the dot-com world, a young Jewish man named Eric who hadn't been to temple in years. A full year into a relationship with a similarly lapsed Christian woman, he found himself yanked back into a state of mind he thought he had abandoned for good. Although Eric claims he has no religious beliefs whatsoever, he felt oddly repulsed by the idea of decorating the Christmas tree that his girlfriend had erected in their apartment. He agreed to let her keep the tree, but he refused to help her apply the tinsel and ornaments. He wouldn't admit it had anything to do with religion.

"I have no religious beliefs," he insisted. "That's why I won't take part. It's your thing."

"But that's a religion, too!" she scolded him. "Your refusal to help is a religion, too."

They fought well into the night, and Eric finally had to concede her point. His refusal to partake of Christmas decorating was a question not of time or taste, but a deeply felt aversion. Inwardly, he was identifying an act he understood as profane and separating himself from it. He was maintaining a cultivated *halakhah* as Jewishly particular as distinguishing between *treyf* and kosher meat. Eric felt he had no religious beliefs, because he didn't experience his own beliefs as religious—only those of his girlfriend. To Eric, the notion of religion itself smacked of superstition and ignorant piety. His own beliefs were just, well, beliefs.

As he recounted the story to me the next day, however, Eric became aware of the fact that his dogmatic refusal to adorn a Christmas tree stemmed from the idol-smashing stories he had been told in Hebrew school as a youngster. And as he allowed himself to accept his own iconoclasm, he found himself extending it into a kind of monotheism.

"Doesn't the Ten Commandments say not to bow down to false idols?" he asked. "I mean, I don't believe in God per se, but I certainly don't believe in gods like Jesus or symbols like Christmas trees!"

"Why do you find other people's gods and icons so distasteful?" I asked him. "Can't people believe in messiahs or trees?"

"Yeah, they can. But I won't." He espoused admirable tolerance and pluralism but kept others' practices at arm's length all the same. "Christmas has gotten insane. People get obsessed with presents and trees and lose sight of each other."

With only the faintest awareness that his belief system had been forged in the classroom of a Reform synagogue, Eric had nonetheless recounted the three crucial building blocks of Jewish theology. Moreover, he discovered them in logical progression, much in the way they were developed by Israelites over time. Iconoclasm leads to the conclusion that any God must, ultimately, be a universal and nameless God. The natural result of settling for an abstract and unknowable deity is to then focus, instead, on human beings and life itself as the supremely sacred vessels of existence. There's no one around to pray to, so one learns to enact sanctity through ethical behavior. Iconoclasm destroys all man-made symbols and leads to abstract monotheism, which in turn leads to an ethos of social justice.

The three primary Jewish values are interdependent, growing into and out of one another so that they become inseparable—almost indistinguishable. Invented in the throes of exile and confirmed by centuries of persecution, these values form the basis of a practical theology. Amazingly, most Jews today don't even know it exists, much less that it informs so many of their beliefs and behaviors.

THE IDOL SMASHERS

Although the Torah's leading cast in order of appearance starts with Adam and then Noah, most people recognize Abraham as the real father of the Jewish people. The first proto-Jew. And as surely as the name George Washington calls to mind a young boy chopping down a cherry tree and then confessing to his father, "I cannot tell a lie," the name Abraham conjures a boy smashing the idols in his father's shop, incapable of understanding how these stone statues could possibly protect someone if they can't even protect themselves.

The story doesn't even come from the Torah; it comes from the midrash—a collection of commentaries and subplots devised by rabbis over subsequent centuries. But it has risen to the level of scripture in the eyes of most Jews because it presents Abraham in his role as counterculture's first and archetypal hero, smashing the conventional icons of his day in order to seed a revolutionary new civilization.

What made Abraham's God such a radical departure from those who went before? The legend of the near sacrifice of his son Isaac, sadly misrepresented to this day, explains the evolutionary leap that iconoclasm makes possible. Although shrouded in apologetic revisionism, some archaeological research and the Torah itself admits to the widespread biblical-era practice of child sacrifice. In fear of the pagan gods—most commonly Molloch—early Canaanites are believed to have sacrificed their firstborn male children on the altar. Though surely a painful process, it was believed that the first male child belonged to the reigning deity and that he must be surrendered lest terrible misfortune befall his father. All later children belonged to the father.*

When biblical Abraham hears the voice of God tell him to sacrifice his son, he has no choice and dutifully—some argue even mechanically—brings Isaac to the altar. But, unlike the pagan fertility gods, Abraham's deity sends an angel to stay his hand. This new God, it is later revealed, requires only the sym-

---

* Of course Isaac was not the firstborn male son, but the second—after Ishmael, who ended up becoming the mythic patriarch of the Egyptian civilization. The many first and second sons in the Torah, as well as their confusing transpositions, are probably best understood as a symbolic way of representing Egypt and Israel, the first- and second-"born" civilizations of the region.

bolic gesture of circumcision to sanctify his covenant. That, and the occasional sacrifice of animals. Though circumcision itself may seem like a cruel punishment to inflict on a hapless infant, it's certainly less barbaric than wholesale slaughter.

Of course, it is not God who requires sacrifices, but man. Fearful of the elements and their chaotic unpredictability, primitive men represented the forces of nature as brooding, angry deities, hungry for a pound of flesh. Further, as Sigmund Freud would later suggest, the birth of a male son represented a threat to the family patriarch and a rival for his wife's affections. These anxieties combined to make child sacrifice a traumatic but oddly reassuring ritual. It seems to have been widespread and recurrent, rising in popularity repeatedly throughout biblical times, as evidenced by how many prophets felt the need to speak out against it. The myth of God's covenant with Abraham was meant to end this barbaric and debilitating practice (killing male sons is a terrible military strategy, to say the least), while replacing it with a relatively harmless ritual that, nonetheless, gave primitive men a way of expressing their anxiety about the wrath of God and the unseen forces of nature and exercising absolute power over their sons. By smashing idols, Abraham made way for an abstract and infinitely more compassionate deity, as well as a set of more humane ways to demonstrate one's devotion to him.

The Exodus story, too—arguably the foundation myth of the Israelites—recounts the abandonment of an idolatrous faith. It must be understood that the legend of Israelite captivity and escape from bondage is not a historical record, but a symbolic emergence from the death cults of Egypt—a metaphoric "rebirth" through the parting waters of the Red Sea. The evidence of a mass migration of Israelites from Goshen is scarce, to say the least. And the story itself, as it would have been accepted by the desert tribes, is of a highly allegorical nature. The Hebrew word for Egypt, Mitzrayim, means "Narrow Place." The slavery from which these people were emerging was not merely the indentured servitude following the great famine, but an enslaved and narrow state of mind.

The Egyptian religion focused on death. Its great monuments—the Pyramids, which required so much labor—were themselves tombs. If some of the allied tribes in the desert did indeed emerge from Egypt, then they surely would have been worshipers of the Egyptian gods. The plagues so painstakingly detailed in the Torah and again each Passover in the Haggadah were understood not as physical attacks on the Egyptian people, but, rather, as symbolic desecrations of their many gods. Blood desecrates the Nile, which was worshiped as a god. Locusts desecrate the corn god, and so on. Each of these gods must be symbolically blasphemed in order to abandon all of them. These were not merely the Egyptians' gods, but those of the pre-Judaic workers, as well.

The final plague, slaying of the firstborn, symbolizes the abandonment of child sacrifice. And how did the Jews avoid this plague themselves? By sacrificing a most sacred Egyptian god, the lamb or goat. The animal god would normally be worshiped as part of the New Year's festivities, celebrated by the Egyptians during April planting season. Instead of worshiping a lamb, the Hebrews of the Exodus myth sacrificed one. It was illegal to kill lambs in ancient Egypt! To paint one's door with lamb's blood, especially at this moment in the year, could only be understood as the ultimate blasphemy against the conventional gods. It was an act of defiance and revolution.

The slaying of the firstborn also represents the fall of the firstborn civilization. Throughout the Torah, it is firstborn sons who meet terrible fates and their younger brothers who carry on the Israelite civilization. From Cain and Ishmael to Esau and Reuben, firstborn sons in the Torah get a bum deal, missing out on blessings, enduring God's wrath, and getting banished. But to early Israelites who understood that Egypt was the firstborn civilization, the elevation of the second-born son symbolized the ascendance of their emergent new society.

What distinguished the Torah's younger sons, and the Hebrews, was that they were shepherds living among farmers. The Torah is the mythic chronicle of the rejection of the early agrarian society as well as the gods and pagan rites on which it depended. Cain, a farmer, sacrificed corn to God, while Abel, a shepherd, sacrificed an animal. Only Abel's was accepted by the Hebrew God. Cain represented the land-based cultures who still prayed to their gods for good weather, while Abel represented the more migrant early Hebrews. It's not that God hates farmers. This myth, and the many others like it, meant to encourage a more abstract spiritual sensibility that wasn't based on a fear of nature's unpredictability, to which primitive farmers were particularly susceptible. These were myths for a new era.

By 700 B.C.E., the axial age had begun, and people already had more food than they needed. They had more leisure time, more time to think, and they began to experience the joys and challenges of an interior life. Their conception of God, too, became more internal and abstract. The bravest among them began to question the social injustices inherent to an agrarian society, including the labor of peasants to support local kings and the huge sacrifices required by local priests. Markets and cities grew in importance, trivializing the supremacy of highly parochial gods.

Even before their exile, Israelites were itinerant people, moving from place to place to feed their stock. Unlike the pagan peoples they encountered, they did not depend on the whims of local gods, nor did they feel the need to placate them at every turn. They were already predisposed to iconoclasm, and they developed myths that supported them in their challenge to conventional, localized worship and helped them resist the nostalgic tug of these more idolatrous sentiments. The Torah is the culmination of this revolutionary axial age outlook.

Israelite spiritual practices were also designed to help

them maintain their iconoclasm. The *Sh'ma* prayer, now taken as a blanket assertion of the unity of God's creation, actually translates to "The Lord is one, alone." It is not merely an exaltation of monotheism, but an explicit negation of the idols, chaos, and polytheism characterizing earlier forms of worship. Why should people have needed to state that they would worship only this abstract God, alone, if he wasn't still in competition with many others? The *Sh'ma* functioned not just as adulation, but also as iconoclasm.

Likewise, rules for the construction of the Ark of the Covenant reveal just how prone early Israelites were to idol worship. Fresh from Egypt, the escaped Israelites of the story are just itching to build and worship something. They were builders after all, and this is what they knew best. The Ark they are told to build is indistinguishable from those still found standing in the ruins of ancient Egypt, except for two telling details. On the top of each Egyptian monument sits a statue of the deity being exalted. According to the instructions received by Moses in the desert, this space is to be left conspicuously empty. Instead, two cherubs—not the sweet flying babies we think of, but huge, scary, faceless monsters—are to be placed on either side of this gap. Their positioning accentuates the absence of an idol, while guarding that space and preventing one from ever being placed there.

In addition, an Egyptian monument would traditionally contain the remains of an important priest or king. The

Hebrews' ark was to be filled instead with the "sacred frag-ments" of the first tablets brought by Moses down Mount Sinai. It is not the dead that are to be exalted; it is the laws of conduct guaranteeing social justice to all.

Similarly, throughout the stories recounted on holidays, Jews are cast as the "stiff-necked people" who can't bring themselves to bow down to anyone or anything. While this term, in Torah, often refers to the Israelites' paralyzing stub-bornness, it also betrays a deeply seated iconoclasm. From Passover to Purim, Jewish holidays celebrate heroes who would rather die than kneel before man or icon. This aversion to idolatry is instilled in Jews incessantly. No wonder Eric couldn't bring himself to decorate a Christmas tree.

ONE FOR ALL, OR ALL FOR ONE?

Their strict iconoclasm makes abstract monotheism Jews' only possible relationship to deity. Any representation of God, even a mental image or pronounceable name, is akin to an idol. This is why no one ever sees God, not even in the Torah. Moses himself is granted only a glimpse of God's *kavod* (holy essence), or afterglow, from the protection of a huge boulder. This singular exception to the rule serves more to underscore the impossibility of gazing upon God's counte-nance than to extol Moses' superhuman ability to sneak a peek.

To worship a single God as unknowable as Moses' Yahweh was a leap for early Israelites. They were an amalgamation of disparate local tribes, each with its own polytheistic scheme. As many religious historians, especially Karen Armstrong in her *History of God,* have chronicled, the Jews needed to be brought into monotheism one step at a time. God's evolution over the course of the Bible, rather than reflecting his character development, traces Jews' growing ability to accept an abstract, withdrawn deity. This process may not yet be complete.

The first step was simply to worship Yahweh as the best and strongest of all the gods out there. Israelites were not required to abandon their underlying polytheism. They needed only promise their loyalty to *this* God above the others. The covenant ceremony itself, as conducted in the Torah by Joshua after the conquest of Canaan, demands that the members of this new federation of tribes worship Yahweh and no one else. He proved himself a more effective deity than those of their vanquished foes and thus earned their devotion.

The linguistic structure of the covenant would have been recognized by anyone of the period as the terms of surrender entered into at the conclusion of a war. The Jews were at once declaring their God victorious over all others and surrendering to him themselves. By granting God the credit for their existence and sustenance, they sought to earn his protection.

Throughout the Bible, the scribes acknowledge the existence of other deities. In Psalm 82, Yahweh actually competes with gods at a "divine assembly" for leadership over mankind. Many other gods exist alongside him, recognized by the psalmist as "divine beings," but Yahweh's claim to superiority over them is his singular dedication to social justice. Even the miracles God performs in the Torah would have been understood by ancient audiences as the typical actions of their former gods. The Canaanite gods were parting the seas all the time—often as part of a fertility myth. It was a classic. Yahweh's parting of the Red Sea is unique only in that he was performing a miracle in order to enact social justice. He was liberating an oppressed people.

God slowly developed from best of gods to the one and only God, as his followers developed their capacity to comprehend such a deity. The God of Abraham makes no claim to being the only God. He is simply the only God who does not demand child sacrifice and the only God willing to negotiate, as he famously does with Abraham. The God of Moses, as depicted in the First Commandment, is a God who will help his people win their wars if they show him sole devotion.

By the time of the prophets, however, the Israelites were losing their wars. The Assyrians had annexed the Northern Kingdom and deported ten of the twelve tribes by 722 B.C.E. The Israelites were facing annihilation. What kind of God could allow this? The prophets Isaiah and Amos evolved the Jewish conception of God to include such a possibility. God was no longer the deity who helped the Israelites against other peoples with other gods, no matter what. He was the only God who existed, and he actually used other peoples to teach the Israelites a lesson when they needed it. The conquering Assyrians were to be understood as instruments of the one and only God.

This is an interesting turn. In the past, God had always earned the Israelites' devotion by performing great acts, taking them out of Egypt or vanquishing their enemies. Now they were supposed to show devotion to a God who not only allowed but purposefully enabled their enemies to conquer them.

The prophets justified this assertion, using a primitive form of what psychologists would call "regression" and "transference." The prophets explained that God was a parent and that his special Israelite children had done some awfully bad things. Isaiah chided them for favoring the wealthy in the Temple, while Hosea assailed them for their frequent reversion to cultic practices. Now God was angry, the prophets said, and he would use the Assyrians to force the Israelites to see the error of their ways.

Devotion to the prophets' more parental God could no longer be shown through external symbols such as expensive sacrifices or gilded statues. The prophets instead stressed social ideals and compassion. The worship of God had to be integrated into the activities of real life. If all people are children in God's family, then the way they behave toward one another is the most important thing to their heavenly father. God no longer took direct actions, as he did back in Exodus, but used his children—the people of all nations—to teach one another. God had receded.

In order to experience this God's reality, his children would have to stop looking for outward signs and, instead, turn inward. There is some evidence that the prophets borrowed this new, internalized concept of God from their Hindu neighbors of the north, who had just a century earlier developed a principle called *atman*. *Atman,* as described in the Upanishads, is the eternal sustaining essence within every individual human being. Godhood is not embodied by some kind of creature or independently existing "God" but is to be found in all things.

The prophets didn't help Israel survive as a kingdom, but they did help the Israeli people preserve their evolving relationship to Yahweh. By adopting this more pervasive and abstract conception of God, the Jews enabled themselves to survive the eventual destruction of the First Temple in 586 B.C.E. and develop a path of devotion that could follow them into exile. Gods had always been associated with places. The prophets of the exile, such as Jeremiah, embraced a new, location-independent idea of God. God is within the individual; he can exist in the heart of any believer. In one of Jeremiah's visions, he describes God handing him a scroll and saying, "Deep within them I will plant my law."

This internalized and all-consuming experience of a truly abstract God allowed the exiled Israelites to distinguish themselves from the people among whom they were now living. As Second Isaiah explained it, Yahweh was not simply the best of all existing gods, but the *only* God. According to most biblical scholars, it was only then that the Torah was amended to include a creation myth. For if Yahweh was indeed the only God who ever was, then he needed to be credited with the formation of the entire universe.

With their newfound monopoly on God, later prophets and scribes were free to reinterpret deity according to their highest ideals. The implications of their abstract conceptions of God are challenging even to modern Jews and ultimately suggest a more metaphoric understanding of the divine. Ezekiel, for example, whose visions detail some of the most bizarre images in biblical literature, always stresses that it "appeared" he was seeing something or "seemed" as though he could hear God. In what are now recognized as the "priestly" additions and revisions to the Bible during this period, God no longer lives in his temple or follows his Israelites through the desert. Just his *kavod,* or essence, fills the empty space in the meeting tent.

By the time of their return to Israel and the rebuilding of the Temple in 522 B.C.E., the Israelites had developed an entirely new way of worshiping through action rather than ritual. The early rabbis compiled their list of the 613 *mitzvot,* or commandments, from the Bible. The new way to live in the presence of God was to carry his spirit into life through the performance of these good deeds. There was no longer a separation between man and God, since man was the vehicle through which God exercised his will. God had no dimension, no body, no specific reality at all. One couldn't look up in the sky to address him. God was everything and everywhere. Since Yahweh was no longer associated with a particular piece of land, many Jews felt no need to return to Israel at all and remained in Babylonia. Instead of bringing sacrifices to the Holy Temple, Jews in Israel and beyond could worship God in a local synagogue through the more inwardly experienced practice of prayer.

The book of Job was rewritten to address this intellectually challenging move into abstractness. In the story, God tests Job's piety through a terrible onslaught of misfortunes. The original version ends with God rewarding Job for his steadfastness. The new version ends much less satisfactorily, with God explaining that Job will never be able to figure out the divine will. It is just too complex—too abstract. Human beings cannot, must not, attempt to conceive of the divine reality.

After 322 B.C.E., Jews within and outside Israel all fell under Greek influence, thanks to the campaigns of Alexander the Great. The Jews and Hellenists had an affinity for each other, each respecting the way logic figured into the other's theology. But while the Greeks were willing to include Yahweh alongside Zeus and Athena in their worship, the Jews held steadfastly to their abstract conception of a single God. The Greeks called the Jews "atheists," seeing godlessness in their abstractions, much as many Christians regard Judaism to this day.

Perhaps the label wasn't (and isn't) altogether wrong. Under Hellenist intellectual influence, Jewish philosopher Philo took God's abstractness to new levels. Seeing no conflict between Greek systems of logic and the Jews' internally directed style of faith, Philo declared that the history of the Bible was entirely allegorical. These stories were meant merely to communicate, metaphorically, an absolutely incomprehensible mystery.

By the time the Romans burned the Second Temple in 70 C.E., many Jewish sects had already decided that the Temple was corrupt anyway. The Pharisees, an extremely spiritual group who lived in ritual purity, preached that Temple rites were unnecessary, favoring prayer through charity and attention to the divine details of existence. Jewish community became the new temple. The emerging talmudic law stressed that God was experienced differently by everybody. Accordingly, the Israelites who witnessed him "directly" at Mount Sinai each saw a different image of God. Likewise, wherever Jews prayed together, the spirit of God was present even though each person experienced him personally and uniquely. There was no longer any official doctrine on what God was. His name could no longer be pronounced; his meaning could no longer be conceived.

From then on, most Jewish thinkers have understood God more by what he is not than by whatever he is. Medieval philosopher Moses Maimonides developed what is now called "negative theology." God is not a creature. God has no hands, and neither does God have emotions. Since any positive attribute of God is "inadmissible," he can be referred to only in the negative. If we are to appreciate God, we must do so by contemplating the underlying order of the natural universe. God is in the beauty of the logic, the details. Maimonides understood that any fixed conception of God must also be a form of idolatry. Negative theology prevents Jews from going backward and reducing their abstract God to a particular image, concept, or icon. But what happens when one moves forward from there?

Let's push the envelope just a little further, along with the existentialist philosophers of the twentieth century: If God cannot be conceived in any way, if his existence is utterly out of the reach of human systems of belief and intellect, then for all practical purposes he does not exist. The evolution of God—from Abraham's fire-breathing warmonger through Moses' righteous savior and Isaiah's compassionate father to Philo's allegorical character in the human drama—is from the real, to the ethereal, to the inconceivable. This is why the spiritual crisis of the twentieth century, precipitated by the success of the scientific model and rationality that came with it, need not threaten one's spiritual foundations. As long as faith finds its foothold in something other than the authority of God or the testaments of those who claim to have encountered him, logic and spirituality are not at odds. God is just not something Jews are supposed to worry about.

In this light, abstract monotheism is not the process by which a people find the one true God, but the path through which they get over their need for him. Whether he exists or not, he is beyond humans' perceptual reach or conceptual grasp. He is increasingly inaccessible and rendered effectively absent. This is no cause for sadness. Our continuing evolution beyond the need for a paternal character named God doesn't mean we have to become atheists; we might just as likely become pantheists, learning to see God in everything and everyone. For at each step along the way, Jews' focus on an external master whose hunger they need to quell or whose edicts they need to obey is replaced by an emphasis on people's duty to one another.

SOCIAL JUSTICE:

NOT DOING UNTO OTHERS

The initial and prime Jewish imperative was never to worship God for his own sake. God doesn't need worship. Jews evolve their concept of him, and their relationship to him, merely as a means toward implementing more humane ways of living.

Noah's God acts through the forces of nature and floods the world in order to start civilization over, on more ethical terms.

Abraham's God speaks directly with man, marking a departure from the bloodlust of his peers, whom many understood as demanding the sacrifice of children and whose decrees were not up for discussion. Moses' God spurns deification through idolatry. He instead sponsors a labor revolt, then crafts a new constitution in the form of the written laws that serve as the foundation of a more just society. The God of the prophets shuns direct worship in favor of a more internally felt divinity, and the God of the talmudic rabbis is satisfied exercising his will through the good conscience of his followers.

God is forever getting out of the way so that people can deal more directly with the real business at hand: making the world a better place in which to live. It's as if the God of the Torah knows that his presence will only be misunderstood, idolized, and exploited. For more primitive and concretized experiences of God almost always lead to human suffering. The Egyptians became so obsessed with religious monuments that they needed slaves to build them. What sort of god would want to be worshiped in that fashion? And how many wars have been fought in what one nation or another believed was "God's name"? The Jewish God's recession from human affairs—and human belief systems—has been all but preordained by the Jewish religion. Slaves neither to sacred icons nor to God's direct decrees, human beings must see one another as worthy of compassion and respect and, in doing so, enact the divine will.

If the stories in the Bible are any indication, that will is dedicated, more than anything else, to social justice. The evolution of Jewish myth and scripture is itself a fossil record of a civilization's development of an ethical template by which to live. It's not an easy template to encapsulate. It is said that when asked by a non-Jew to summarize his religion while standing on one foot, the great talmudic sage Hillel merely said, "What is hateful unto you do not do unto your neighbor. The rest is commentary."

Even in this ultracompressed version of Judaism, Hillel is careful to state himself in the negative. Do *not* do what is hateful. The much better-known inverse, "Do unto others as you would have them do unto you," has an entirely different meaning. It is a particularly dangerous phrase in the mouths of reformers and the Crusaders, who used the positively stated rule to justify the killing of non-Christians. According to their logic, if you yourself would rather be slain at the hands of a righteous man than die a nonbeliever, then you must kill all nonbelievers! Hillel's negative phraseology, like Maimonides's negative theology, keeps any particular command from God out of the equation. It resists misuse by warmongers and violent proselytizers by leaving in doubt just what it is God wants his people to do. It is the work of Jews to figure this out provisionally for every situation. And as long as there is someone being abused or exploited in the world, this work never stops. For someone is being treated in a way Jews *wouldn't* want to be treated themselves.

Social justice, Jewish style, cannot be accomplished by following a blanket decree. The dictates themselves would merely
become the new idols. Jews would end up worshiping the laws
instead of enacting the liberties they were meant to express. In
Judaism, the oral law—the ever-expanding commentaries,
the Talmud and the midrash—are considered just as holy as the
written law given to Moses. It's all from God, even if conceived
and written by people, and all equally valid. Social justice is an
ongoing struggle, with human beings taking equal responsibility for determining just how to keep one another free from
oppression. Though there are many *mitzvot* (commandments) in
the Torah, they don't result in a dictated, positive code of social
and moral behavior. Jews must infer what these best practices
are and actively define them in each moment.

Jewish literature does offer some clues. The Torah inti-
mates the path of righteousness through the lives and experiences of its characters—none of whom get it exactly right.
There *is* no word for "hero" in the Torah. Judaism's mythical
heroes are imperfect people, striving to behave as righteously
as they can figure out. The characters develop their ethical
stances as they go along. Because the ultimate God-ordained
path can never be positively described in Jewish literature, it
must be inferred from the direction in which our great
heroes are attempting to go. None of them exhibit perfection;
that's only for messiahs.

But they do try, and with increasing success. The Torah

itself gives us a great clue in the incremental improvements exhibited by its first three great ethical heroes, Noah, Abraham, and Moses. When God tells Noah that he is about to destroy the world, Noah believes him and dutifully builds an ark to save his family and members of all earth's species. He carries out God's orders but voices not a word of compassion for all the people who are going to be killed. He saves his family, as might be expected of anyone.

The Torah's next hero fares a bit better. When Abraham learns of God's intention to destroy Sodom and Gomorrah, he argues with God on behalf of the "righteous" few who may still dwell in these sinful cities. He makes God agree to spare both communities if ten righteous men can be found among them. It was a good try, but God can't find ten righteous people, so he destroys the cities.

Moses comes the closest. When he learns of God's intention to destroy the Israelites for worshiping the golden calf they have built at Mount Sinai, he does more than negotiate with words: he offers his own life in their stead. Only this measure of compassionate self-sacrifice is enough to sway God, who then spares his people.

Noah worked to save his own family. Abraham bargained to save the righteous. Moses was willing to lay down his own life for sinners. This progression implies successively higher forms of compassion, with increasing personal risks. Jews' sense of social justice is supposed to extend past the family and even the worthy, to include all people.

Moses' development as an individual follows the same progression. He is first inspired to act on behalf of another human being when he witnesses a slave being beaten by an Egyptian guard. To save this man's life, he slays the guard. One line later in the biblical narrative, he is again moved to take action when he witnesses two Israelite slaves fighting. One of them asks sarcastically if Moses is going to kill him, too, as he did that guard the day before. Realizing that news of his murder is spreading fast, Moses leaves town, only to come upon several Midianite sisters being deprived of their rights to water their horses at a local well. Again, he intercedes on their behalf.

The three incidents, occurring in the same short paragraph, trace the development of Moses' instinct for justice. In the first instance, he saves an Israelite—one of his own people, according to legend—from an Egyptian. In the second, he saves one Israelite from another. In the third, he intercedes on behalf of a stranger. His sense of social justice is expanding. His definition of justice is also becoming more inclusive and subtle. He first acts when someone is in danger of losing his life. Then he takes action when the threat is physical, but certainly not lethal. Finally he stands up for people whose property rights are being denied them. All are injustices, to be sure, but their progression from murderous cruelty to economic injustice, and from stranger against kinsman to stranger against stranger, is more than coincidental. They show how for Jews, the definition of social justice has an ever-expanding radius.

The mandate to care for strangers as Jews would care for themselves or, more specifically, to not allow anything to be done toward a stranger that they wouldn't want done toward themselves is echoed not just once, but over forty separate times in Torah as God reminds his people, "You must not oppress the stranger; you know how a stranger feels, for you lived as strangers in the land of Egypt." The Jewish mandate for social justice, as learned through collective mythic experience and as evolved by the Torah's most heroic characters, reaches its highest ideals when one takes action to prevent the exploitation of strangers.

Jewish holidays also teach, through allegory, how to turn one's experiences and mythologies into opportunities for social justice. Although most Jewish festivals are themselves based on more ancient pagan rites, their Jewish incarnations invariably reinterpret them as celebrations of human rights victories. The slaying of the lamb, repurposed as a component of the Passover ritual, becomes the symbol of Jewish liberation from a pharaoh who had regularly slain their sons. The Purim story, itself a derivative of the Persian fertility rites for Marduk and Ishtar, becomes the legend of Mordechai and Esther's revolt against an unjust prime minister, Haman. The seventh-day quarter-moon festival is refashioned into Shabbat, a day of rest for slaves who had no previous concept of labor laws. In each case, the holidays become more specifically Jewish as they are reinterpreted in the light of an evolving humanitarian sensibility.

Like the holy texts and the tales of the patriarchs, Jewish holidays are meant to instill, above all else, a sense of compassion as well as an impulse to act upon it on behalf of Jews and strangers alike. Subsequent Jewish inventions survive only as long as they are able to fit into this greater scheme of social justice. The medieval concept of *tikkun olam,* or "healing the earth," was born out of the exilic experience of isolation from God. Jews were being persecuted, murdered, and expelled from every nation in Europe. Mystics had developed a reassuring myth explaining that the Jews' sense of despair came from the fact that the universe was "broken," leaving Jews separated from their loving God. One day, in the messianic age, the cleft would be healed. As it is understood today, however, *tikkun olam* is just a poetic way of expressing the responsibility Jews have to "heal the earth." What began as a consoling mystical fable can't help but evolve into yet another mandate for social justice on behalf of the whole planet.

SHARING THE FRUIT:

JEWISH ACTIVISM

The three pillars of the Jewish faith, iconoclasm, abstract monotheism, and social justice, have resulted in a people whose very character was defined by a willingness to engage themselves in the plights of others. Although the very best evidence of the Jewish struggle for social justice has occurred only in recent centuries, as American Jews have had the luxury of limited persecution, Jewish law and culture is nonetheless permeated by the duty of social justice in many forms.

The Jewish word for charity, *tzedakah,* actually means "justice." It is not enough to give money to the poor; a Jew's actions must actually work to increase the amount of justice in the world. The Jewish term *pe'a*—from which is derived the word *payess* (those little curls descending from Hasidic sideburns)—refers to the practice of leaving a corner of the field and portion of one's crops for the poor. *Leket,* or gleanings, refers to the fruits and vegetables that fall to the ground during harvest, which must also be left for the poor, along with *shik'ha,* the intentionally unpicked sheaves of corn. This tithing was considered not charity, but a duty.

Jews institutionalized a number of other measures meant to promote economic justice. After every seven-year cycle, all debts were to be forgiven—giving every person the opportunity to achieve a "clean slate." As a way of keeping ego out of *tzedakah,* as well as keeping shame out of accepting it, special chambers were created in the Second Temple that allowed the wealthy to leave donations through one entrance while the poor could collect them, unseen, via another. It was considered better not to give than to give in a way that humiliated the receiver. Further, following a dictate in Deuteronomy, Jews were not allowed to overwork their laborers, and judges were required to give employees the benefit of the doubt in labor disputes, since it is more likely that the employer will have forgotten the facts of the incident.

By the first and second centuries C.E., Jews developed the idea of community soup kitchens, called *tamhu'i,* and relief funds for the poor, called *kuppah.* Another fund, called *arnak shel tzedakah,* was collected specifically for the benefit of orphans. Jews appointed charity wardens, who collected money from all Jewish citizens and then distributed regular living allowances to the poor. The Talmud (in TB Sanhedrin 17b) specifically forbids scholars from living in a town that does not have a functioning *kuppah.* Likewise, festivals and celebrations were not allowed to begin until all the hungry who had come—Jew and non-Jew—were seated and fed.

These practices remained fairly unchanged through almost two millennia of Jewish life in segregated shtetls and ghettos. Although Jewish thinkers were seminal in the development of republicanism, the Enlightenment, and socialism, the Jews were usually persecuted or expelled by their host nations once such movements gathered steam. As one of the many voices from Jewish history in *Life Is with People* recounts, "Life in the shtetl begins and ends with tzedaka. When a child is born, the father pledges a certain amount of money for distribution to the poor. At a funeral the mourners distribute coins to the beggars who swarm the cemetery. . . . If something good or bad happens, one puts a coin into the box."

Of course, Jewish social justice on a grand scale could not take place until Jews had enough education for themselves, and interaction with open-minded Europeans, to be able to influence national and global events. In many cases, Jews were able to extend their ethical practices outside the shtetl only by fighting for some justice for themselves first.

Most of the major players in the Communist revolution against the oppressive czarist regime—including Trotsky, Sverdlov, Zinoviev, Radek, Litvinov, and Kamenev—were Jews. True enough, Russian Jews had experienced as much as anyone the oppressive yoke of Peter's rule, and scores had died in the state-sponsored pogroms against their communities. But they were not alone in their suffering, and their suffering alone did not account for their ability to envision, if not successfully implement, a more just social order. And neither does local oppression explain the huge number of American Jews who gave financial support for their cause.

American Jews have since earned a reputation for espousing "leftie" liberal values, voting democratic, and fighting on behalf of oppressed laborers and minorities. This is not an unfounded stereotype, and the evidence of Jewish involvement in socially progressive causes is much more than anecdotal. The numbers and facts bear this out.

Jews were responsible for launching the labor movement

here in America, much to their own peril. Samuel Gompers cofounded then served as the first president of the American Federation of Labor, the dominant organizing force in the early labor actions of the United States and Canada. Worker and activist Clara Lemlich launched a series of strikes against sweatshops in 1909. Her organizational efforts and famously rousing speeches gained national attention after the 1911 Triangle Shirtwaist Factory fire killed 146 people in fifteen minutes, most of them young Jewish women. By 1934, a newly formed Jewish Labor Committee led the cry against oppressive conditions for garment and other workers and began negotiating the first modern labor laws.

It has been argued that early Jewish labor activism, however noble, was a primarily self-serving social and political enterprise, because there were many Jews among the immigrant laborers being fought for. What this analysis misses, however, is that once they were unionized, Americanized, and safe in their own status as upwardly mobile citizens, Jews immediately expanded their activism, devoting themselves to the universal fight for civil liberties.

After World War II, Jewish agencies (many of which had been formed explicitly for self-preservation) came to understand the problem of anti-Semitism as part of a larger epidemic of prejudice and discrimination. Groups including the Anti-Defamation League funded an enormous wave of scholastic sociological research, educational programs, media campaigns, and conferences. The 1950 *Studies in Prejudice* series, documenting the research of a group of scientists and academics sponsored by the American Jewish Committee, changed the accepted definition of prejudice from a "psychological disorder" to a conscious social and political choice. Viewing prejudice as a form of intellectual and emotional confusion fueled by ignorance and a sense of threat, Jewish groups hoped to change American attitudes through education and open discussion.

When media-based strategies proved unsuccessful, American Jewish agencies used their organized power for legal action. The American Jewish Congress's Commission on Law and Social Action (CLSA) drafted many of the civil rights bills that eventually became laws. Joseph Robinson, who directed the commission's northeast division, became a national authority on civil rights, and his office grew into a hub of activism. In 1948, the CLSA-sponsored Quinn-Olliffe bill, passed in New York State, was the first U.S. law to ban the unfair refusal of a qualified college applicant based on race, color, creed, or national origin. In 1952, the American Jewish Congress worked with the National Association for the Advancement of Colored People (NAACP) to target unfair housing policy. Through a series of legal battles, American Jewish Congress attorneys ended the whites-only policy of New York City's Stuyvesant Town, setting an important legal precedent against discrimination in housing projects that received any amount of public aid.

Remembering how "strangers feel in a strange land," Jews saw their own ancient history in the plight of former American slaves and put their lives on the line for a cause they saw not merely as just, but required. In 1909, Jews helped organize and fund the NAACP, with heroes such as J. Rosenthal, Lillian Wald, H. Malkewitz, and Rabbi E. Hirsch embarking on a controversial alliance with African American W. E. B. Dubois. By 1964, Jews made up over half of the white volunteers who went to Mississippi to protest the Jim Crow laws in the famous "Mississippi Burning" saga. No less than 50 percent of civil rights lawyers in the South were Jewish. And, breaking with tradition that "religious Jews" not involve themselves directly in politics and instead leave such matters to their secular counterparts, Rabbi Abraham Joshua Heschel marched arm in arm with Martin Luther King, demonstrating for the world that the cause of African Americans was now central to Judaism. Jewish theology could not coexist with such blatant oppression and required that even rabbis champion the cause of civil rights as an essential component of practicing their faith.

Heschel's move stirred much controversy in Jewish circles. Jews had always been political, but rabbis were supposed to be sitting in shul contemplating the holy books. This false distinction cost Jewish institutions dearly. As Jewish activists flocked to the sides of their African American counterparts, temples, federations, and other solely Jewish-identified organizations were left to languish. The reaction of far-thinking Jews to universal injustice caused a split between those who sought to conduct true outreach and those whose concerns were more insular. The inward focus of Jews who stayed behind to man the fort was only exacerbated by what they saw as the mass exodus by Jews to the concerns of others. Ironically, they came to depend on crises in Israel, such as the Six-Day War, for their ability to galvanize Jewish support for Jewish-specific causes. It was an equation for disaster.

Just as the definition of social justice had to evolve over time, so must the definition of what it means to be Jewish. The ever-expanding circle of Jewish concerns was designed to embrace, not exclude, Judaism's high-minded members in their exploits on behalf of the world at large. Instead, Jews who pursued careers in social justice, or who dedicated their lives to the most universally progressive ideals, became known as "lapsed" Jews. They were busy forming the American Civil Liberties Union (ACLU), Legal Aid societies, and international relief efforts. Though they had merely followed the same path as Moses toward unbiased compassion and selfless activism, they had seemingly abandoned all that was nominally Jewish. Now, Jewish "outreach" efforts are spending millions of dollars each year in a misguided effort get them "back."

This is hardly a sturdy foundation from which to extend the

fruits of iconoclasm, abstract monotheism, and social justice to a world facing the challenges of closed-minded fundamentalism and the anxieties associated with globalization.

This so-called lapsed constituency might actually comprise Judaism's most devoutly practicing members. It is not these people, but what is considered "Jewish" that needs to change.

Two

HOW WE LOST
THE PLOT

I WAS VISITING MY GRANDMOTHER at her Boca Raton re-
tirement village one weekend last winter, and I asked her if she
wanted to go to synagogue on Shabbat morning. I'd been going every weekend in preparation for writing this book, and
I thought my grandmother would be pleased, or at least
amused, by my invitation.

"No," she exclaimed, "I won't go in there!" I asked her
why. "They parade that Torah around like it's an idol," she
said. "And then they make you kiss it. It's against my religion!"

Ninety-seven this year, Sabina is not your typical Jewish
grandmother. Come to think of it, maybe she *is* typical of her
generation. Don't all American Jews have a die-hard Communist in the family somewhere? Sabina grew up on New York's

Lower East Side, just two blocks from where I've ended up living today. I take yoga classes in the same brownstone that once
served as her family's shul! Her parents vacationed with her at
a Communist camp in upstate New York run by the Workmen's
Circle ("It was the only place cheap enough we could go"), and
by the early 1920s, teenage Sabina was marching, along with
hundreds of other Jews, behind union pioneer Eugene Debs.

Sabina's brand of Judaism is more grounded in iconoclasm, end-stage monotheism, and social justice than it is in
faith. She feels most Jewish when she is voting for Democrats
or raising funds for Hadassah. She doesn't even believe in
God—"He's just another way to keep the masses in line," she
likes to say—but prefers to see the godly in everyone. Still, her
principles are, in many ways, more Jewish than what is being
practiced in the temple where she refuses to worship. How has
Judaism gotten itself into a situation where a Jewish woman
feels that walking into a synagogue is against her religion?

Even more puzzling to me, when I told Sabina about my
intention to write this book, she advised me to try another subject.
Sure, she agreed, the kinds of questions I am asking are legitimate, even important. But they're not for public consumption.

"These are dangerous ideas," she said, "even if they happen to be right." Things for Jews and Israel are "bad enough
already."

I protested. How could she, of all people, tell me to keep a
lid on the truth? As she well knows, Judaism is in dire need of

a revolution of its own. Don't we need to face up to where we've gone wrong and how our institutions no longer support the brilliant ideas they were created to protect?

"You want to say bad things about the Jews, that anyone can read and then use against us? Leave it alone."

Back and forth we went, me arguing for a good hard look at the Jewish dilemma and Sabina telling me I was overestimating our ability as a people to withstand such an interrogation—particularly in front of outsiders who are just looking for an excuse to revive old prejudices.

"You don't know what we've been through," she explained. "You think things are good. You think we're all safe. And that's when it happens."

"When what happens? Another Holocaust? Come on!"

She just shrugged.

"All I want to do is help people ask the right questions, Grandma."

"Ask yourself just one question, my darling," she said, picking up her remote and turning on the evening news. "Is it good for the Jews?"

WRESTLING WITH GOD

Today's Jews are not taught in Hebrew school that many of our holidays are based on those of previous civilizations. Or that the Torah was written and rewritten over a period of centuries by rabbis and even politicians. Or that many events in the Bible are allegorical and not historically accurate. Some of us have been taught the very opposite, and in some cases by teachers and rabbis who knew that what they were preaching wasn't true. All because they believed such obfuscation was "good for the Jews."

By refusing to continue the spirit of inquiry that has characterized Jewish thought for two millennia, we are robbing ourselves of the very tools that empower us to face the many challenges we encounter as Jews. It is, admittedly, because we are one of the world's most thoughtfully inquisitive civilizations that we run into so much trouble. However, retreating into voluntary passivity and numb acceptance of hand-me-down decrees is an act not of self-preservation, but of self-annihilation. In the name of Judaism, we suppress the Jewish.

What is a Jew or, more precisely, an Israelite? "Jew" is actually a misnomer, a word used to identify the people of Judea—the sole surviving kingdom of Israel after the Assyrian invasion. Israelites are the people who claim Jacob as their spiritual patriarch. Jacob, whose name means "Trickster," stole Esau's birthright from their blind father, Isaac, by putting a goatskin on his arms to make them feel more like his brother's. His name was changed to Israel only after a long night of battling his own bad conscience for what he'd done, in the personage of an angel sent by God. Jacob becomes Israel not by hearing the word of God, but by wrestling with him. Since Jacob awakes from his dream alone but physically injured, it has been suggested that his long night of wrestling with God was actually a battle with himself.

The faith of Israel, then—what we call Judaism—was born not out of the acceptance of a belief, but out of a willingness to challenge one's beliefs. It was by confronting the darkest regions of his conscience, and committing to do battle with his perception of God, that Jacob elevated himself to become the first true Israelite. Likewise, it is by facing the reality of our heritage, experiencing the mixed blessing of our unique relationship to divinity, and then wrestling with everything we call sacred that we genuinely carry on the tradition our mythic patriarchs left us as our legacy. What is Judaism, after all, if not the willingness to ask questions?

So far, most of the rabbis I've met in my travels either refuse to take up this challenge or refuse to believe that we laypeople can handle it. Last year, I delivered a talk to a congregation in Manhattan, made up mostly of high-tech entrepreneurs who had recently returned to Judaism, in which I referred to the mythological underpinnings of the Torah. I explained how Judaism is characterized by iconoclasm and demonstrated the way that early Jews would have understood the idols desecrated by the symbolic ten plagues of Exodus. When I was done, I noticed that the rabbi had turned beet red.

"Those are some very interesting notions," he said as he retook the pulpit and the microphone. "But even you must agree that God wrote the Torah."

"Well," I countered, thinking fast, "I'm a radical monotheist. In that sense, what book *didn't* God write?" Too flippant.

"Indeed," he said, grasping the lectern with both hands, "I just want to reassure everyone here that these kinds of ideas—while useful in debates at the seminary—are radical and unfounded. We now have archaeological proof that all the events in the Torah happened exactly as described."

Several members of the congregation smiled and nodded. He went on confidently, "Judaism may be iconoclastic, but some icons are better left as icons." As Jews, he explained, we must take some things on faith.

I was incensed. This rabbi was turning Judaism into a set of sacred and inviolable truths. He was sacrificing our iconoclasm, our abstract monotheism, and our community-driven ethos to an oversimplified set of pat answers that were to be accepted on faith. Intelligent inquiry, textual literacy, and genuine engagement were to be surrendered. And this rabbi truly believed he was doing a good thing. He thought he was saving a religion.

Amazingly, when we spoke alone together later, the rabbi admitted that everything I had told his congregation was basically correct. He was not a stupid man and had been educated in the historical and theological foundations of Judaism. He simply believed that his congregants were not ready or willing to engage with their religion in the manner I was proposing. The real issues facing Jews today, he insisted, are assimilation, intermarriage, moral decay, and declining respect for Israel. This was not an appropriate moment to open Judaism to potentially unsettling analysis, but, rather, a time to ingrain more firmly the kinds of beliefs that keep people kissing their mezuzahs and, more important, coming to temple, donating money, and raising Jewish children. Hadn't I seen the numbers?

Yes, I've seen the numbers. Intermarriage is on the rise, and fewer non-Jewish spouses are converting to Judaism than ever before. Intermarried couples are no longer introducing their children to the Jewish faith, and increasing numbers of young people who are raised Jewish abandon the religion shortly after their bar or bat mitzvahs. There are more self-defined "lapsed" Jews than ever, and if something isn't done, the number of practicing Jews will dwindle, within a generation, to an insignificant population.

Instead of reducing Judaism to an easily digested set of platitudes, our religious leaders might be better off looking at why so many people are finding institutional Judaism irrelevant to our daily experience as modern Americans. It may not be that they are overestimating our ability to relate to the complexities of Judaism, but that they have sadly underestimated our need for the real thing.

Maybe we're up for the next round in the good fight that Jacob began.

WHERE WE'RE AT

Although it finds its roots in some of the most progressive ideas conceived in history, Judaism today is nonetheless associated with superstition, racism, sexism, and a haughty refusal to clean up its own act. Look around, and you'll soon understand why Jews and non-Jews alike get this impression of us.

The current landscape of Jewish offerings isn't pretty.

Today, the synagogue is one of the last places healthy, successful people go to engage in the kind of cultural analysis that the modern experience requires of us. The shul I attended until recently is a small, Conservative synagogue in Manhattan, plagued by infighting and politics. In one year two rabbis were fired—the first for appealing too strongly to the gay community, the second for using the new prayer books that had been willed to the congregation by a member who had died of AIDS.

The new prayer books—the Conservative movement's

officially approved text—now included the matriarchs in certain traditional daily prayers that in previous versions had named only their male counterparts. The president of the synagogue, along with several other influential older board members, felt that this modification violated the main purpose of synagogue, which was to preserve, with museumlike accuracy, the rituals of the Jewish people.

It's not an altogether unfounded premise. Jewish ritual has always been a community-decided affair, and different congregations adopt changes at different rates. But the main drive behind this synagogue's intransigence was a kind of nostalgia. Members spoke longingly about the style of religious experiences they imagined their grandparents having back in the shtetls of Eastern Europe. By imitating the outward appearance, and even appropriating the accents of their Yiddish-speaking forebears, these congregants hoped they could reach back to a simpler and more ethical time.

This penchant for nostalgia rendered the shul spiritually ineffectual—absolutely disconnected from the world in which it lived. After each rabbi's premature dismissal, attendance at services dwindled, dues-paying membership decreased, and the synagogue's core constituency found itself increasingly isolated. The worse things got, the more hardened were the synagogue's officers in their commitment to resist the corrosive effects of modernity. Like a cult facing the pressures of the external world, they turned inward and began eyeing potential members with a combination of desperation and suspicion. Whose side would he or she be on? Are they *our kind* of people?

A relative of mine was recently hired as the rabbi of a shul facing a different dilemma. It is a pretty successful suburban synagogue in the midst of a multiyear fund-raising campaign for a new building in a better neighborhood. They hired a consultant, at a cost of four thousand dollars per week, to help them raise more money from their own community—from themselves. The consultant uses every trick in the book, pitting congregants against one another, ostracizing those who refuse to get on board, and creating high-pressure social situations where the size of one's donation decides his place in the community hierarchy.

The rabbi is required to attend these "dinner parties" and to use whatever he knows about each congregant as ammunition in applying the necessary psychological leverage. He doesn't enjoy his work, but it is exactly what he has been hired to do. He hopes that the ends justify the means and that the congregation will be able to "survive the ordeal" he is putting them through.

Another synagogue I visited, in San Francisco, is busy appealing to the scores of "returnees," or what are known as *ba'al teshuvahs,* in search of authentic Judaism. Usually young and professionally successful, returnees are people who have grown to feel that something is missing from their lives. They find their daily occupations unrewarding, even unethical to some degree, and hope to restore a sense of dignity and rightness to their existence by delving headlong into the religion of their parents—not just in nostalgic imitation, but by actually out-*Jewing* them. Though they haven't practiced any Judaism since their bar mitzvahs, if they went even that far in their first go-round, they now want to approximate the rigors of orthodoxy. They separate their dishes into meat and dairy and dutifully place mezuzahs on every door of their homes with varying, and often surprisingly scant, interest in what any of these rituals mean. They tend to care only that they are doing everything "right" and usually interrogate their rabbis on behavioral details such as whether they need two dishwashers or how regularly they need to change the parchment in their tefillin (prayer bindings). Faced with the harrowing ethical complexities of their professional lives, they seem to cling to the performative actions prescribed by the ancient texts as a way of assuaging their guilt and, presumably, the wrath of God.

"At least they're walking in the door," the head rabbi of this Bay Area synagogue catering to returnees told me. "I give them answers to their questions. Someday, maybe they'll ask better ones."

By entertaining the returnees' need for spiritual certainty and ritualistic purity, however, such rabbis are promoting a distorted and potentially idolatrous form of Judaism. Jews who are encouraged in this style of worship tend to see their actions as magical in nature. They believe their mezuzahs provide supernatural protection to their homes and treat them more as powerful talismans than simple reminders. Instead of inviting inquiry and self-appraisal, their mindless worship replaces it. From what I have observed, their practices tend to fill them with self-righteousness and superiority, enabling them to avoid making substantive changes to the factors in their lives that led them to seek spiritual solace in the first place.

While it may not be a rabbi's job to confront congregants on the ethical inconsistencies of their life choices—especially when they are big donors—a spiritual tradition based on honest inquiry is in trouble when it serves to solve its worshipers' ethical quandaries through magical protection.

Nowhere is this more evident than in the kabbalah, or Jewish mysticism movement, now enjoying a terrific comeback thanks to the disillusionment of younger Jews with the sorts of synagogues I've already described, combined with the emergence of a new breed of rabbis who know how to package religion for a modern, New Age audience. Kabbalah schools are springing up throughout America, promising to teach the "secret" truths that rabbis have feared to share with their congregants for centuries. These secrets have nothing to do with the origins of Torah or the development of Jewish law. They concern, instead, speciously derived interpretations of the mysterious and encoded texts and rituals of medieval kabbalists, advertised as containing the keys to great power and protection.

Devotees pay thousands of dollars for multivolume sets of the *Zohar,* an ancient mystical interpretation of Judaism. They don't actually read these books, because they are written in ancient Aramaic. Instead, they are to pass their eyes over the cryptic text and absorb the energy within them. This is a path not of learning, but of divine transmission. As a rabbi from the Kabbalah Learning Center in New York explained it to me, "The mind only gets in the way. The soul can absorb the truth of these texts like a grocery store scanner reads the bar code on a package." The most celebrated rabbis in this newly revived tradition conduct elaborate rituals in which, for a price, they tie a red string around the initiates' wrists. The string is supposed to protect them from the "evil eye." Madonna and other celebrities sported them quite famously at a televised awards ceremony in the late nineties, leading to an increase in attention for the new kabbalah's mystical, and fashionable, set of practices.

The New Age movement offers a wide array of spiritual choices for those fed up with the institutional biases of organized religion. With a mystical movement all their own, kabbalist rabbis can provide a path to those who want the

experiential immediacy of a New Age practice without resorting to a foreign faith like Buddhism and starting from
scratch. Followers get the kick of practicing something that
feels more spiritual than religious, without straying too far
from the faith that has always felt safe. They hope to taste
something spiritual while still getting to be Jewish. Unfortunately, most get neither.

There is certainly evidence of a mystical Judaism dating as
far back as the Second Temple period. Certain sects of early
Jews meditated on God's holy throne, sang hymns that they
hoped would bring them into a state of spiritual ecstasy, and
looked for correlations between Hebrew words, letters, numbers, and their meanings. This activity did not occur in a vac-
uum, however, and was quite consciously and methodically
refocused on the study of Torah. It was really more of a way for
scholars to invigorate their text study with experiential bliss
and insights than it was a substitute for learning or practice.

The courses and services offered by the vast majority of
today's pop-Kabbalists have little to do with learning, experiential or otherwise. These well-marketed and highly captivat-
ing programs find their origins not in the ancient, pre-Judaic
era their promoters claim but instead are loosely based on
a myth developed by a medieval rabbi named Isaac Luria.
Addressing a Jewish constituency in the throes of exile and
inquisition, Luria created an allegory for the exilic experience.

According to the story, in order to create the realm in which human beings live, God was forced to separate from part of himself. The single container of divine energy was broken. Although all human beings live in a dimension that is now separated from God, all Jews have within them a "divine spark" of God's original true essence. The pain and longing of existence is the result of those sparks attempting to reach back to the God from whom Jews were cut off—trying to make the universe whole again. One day, in the messianic age, these sparks will return to the Creator. Luria also broke with tradition by permitting Jews to worship by themselves instead of with a minyan (ten other Jewish men or, in more modern circles, people). He felt that Jews in despair should be able to practice by meditating on their eventual return to the divine source.

Worshiping in such a fashion was not without its downside, for soon the followers of Lurianic kabbalah were interpreting his myth quite literally, believing that redemption and a return to the Promised Land were just around the corner. Many Jews stirred themselves into a messianic frenzy and then succumbed to even greater despair when their messiahs fell short of expectations. Today, the dedication to the myth of kabbalah is also characterized by a desperate longing for return from exile and has found its expression in pop cultural offerings from tattoos depicting the kabbalist path toward

God to rock lyrics celebrating the great unification at the end of time.

It's a beautiful sentiment, to be sure, but it is hardly Jewish, as we've been defining it. Kabbalists are not empowered to act but are implored to wait for better times. By purchasing totems and submitting to mysterious rituals conducted by purportedly awakened beings, the faithful are rewarded with externally granted protection and blessing. They practice alone, without the buffering and grounding influence of a community. They do not analyze text or even understand what it means. They're not supposed to. There is nothing they need to do. The activist, revolutionary stripe of Judaism is satisfied, instead, by the sense that these are practices long forbidden by a legacy of patriarchal sages who monopolized their power for their own ends. The unfortunate tendency of congregations to hold on to some of Judaism's more sexist traditions and prayers has yielded a crop of young, mostly female, discontents now ripe for the harvest. Kabbalah feels cool and controversial. Not your father's Judaism.

The reinvention of Judaism as "cool" is also the aim of philanthropies and outreach organizations that have taken it upon themselves to repackage a religion for a vast population of lapsed and disaffected Jews. Outreach organizations define Jews as people who are affiliated with a Jewish organization. Their efforts fail to take into account the sociological research indicating that modern Americans define their social, political, or religious affiliations not through centralized institutions, but through a more complex and self-defined set of "loose connections." Instead of working to strengthen these connections, most outreach groups think of Jews as being "in" or "out" based on their willingness to pay temple dues. People who don't belong to a synagogue are considered "lapsed" and in need of active recruitment. Through focus groups and consumer research, these organizations seek to identify their target market's barriers to participating in organized Judaism and then appeal to these sensibilities. It all comes down to making Judaism look more hip to modern audiences, even if this means resorting to the tactics of a soft drink advertiser.

What the focus groups found was that most young Jews felt that Judaism and its institutions were stuck in the past. They abhorred the styles and social customs they associated with Judaism, such as gaudy bar mitzvahs and indulgently operatic cantors. To them, Judaism was an immigrant's religion, suitable only for people who didn't feel like real Americans. Sure, some believed in God and even preferred the idea of finding a Jewish marriage partner, but temple was boring; Israel was repressively militaristic; and synagogues themselves were crowded with old people.

If only Judaism were presented in a different, more contemporary package, these outreach groups concluded, perhaps they could attract young people back into the fold. So countless new projects were initiated and funded, all designed to make "Jewishness" a more desirable component of a twenty-something's self-image.

One young man I met, the well-meaning director of a Jewish cultural revitalization campaign, genuinely believed that if only our cultural artifacts were less tacky, more Jews would be able to relate proudly to the faith. His vision of an updated Jewish aesthetic included a seder plate designed by, say, contemporary Jewish artist Barbara Kruger or a menorah fashioned by Frank Gehry. If people only knew that these extraordinarily sophisticated designers were Jewish, he felt, they might be motivated to find out more about the religion itself. At least they would no longer think of Judaism in terms of the ugly, bourgeois styles of their parents from the suburbs.

He invited me and about thirty other young Jews in creative professions to spend a weekend with him and a team of facilitators from a "scenario planning" consultancy to imagine the Jewish future and then devise publications, social events, and cultural institutions that might appeal to the troublesome twenty-something Jewish demographic. We were briefed on their research, on the segments of the target market, and on several possible directions in which Judaism might shift, given different global and economic trends. Our task was, essentially, to make Jewish offerings as compelling as everything else out there, from "Free Tibet" concerts to MTV.

It sounded good at the time, but we all soon learned that the problem with this strategy is that if Jewish cultural offerings are as hip, aspirational, and image-based as everything else in commercial America, then why bother with them? Mightn't spirituality best be a relief from the endless pursuit of cool instead of a celebration of its most intimidating features?

Take Makor, a Manhattan community center designed through focus groups and marketing research to attract upwardly mobile Jewish singles. It's a gorgeous facility—a remodeled town house with a nightclub and restaurant in the basement; a library, lounge, and lecture hall on the first floor; and upper floors dedicated to screening rooms and classes. Its original founder's intentions were to stem intermarriage by providing a comfortable and trendy atmosphere for Jewish singles to meet and, eventually, marry one another instead of gentiles. Makor's events were a bit too popular, however, and soon Jew and gentile alike were attending the jazz concerts and parties there. So the mission and its implementation were revised to focus more directly on Jewish-friendly events, such as a fifty-dollar Purim party where rock star Perry Farrell mixed records, or a debate between a rabbi who writes "kosher" sex books and a Jewish *Playboy* centerfold. Anything to draw a crowd, because once people are in the building, there's the chance for chemistry between them.

The results have been at best exploitative and at worst

pornographic. At the sex debate, for instance, a talk radio host with a penchant for the sensational moderated the proceedings, announcing that we were about to witness a conversation between "the rabbi and the centerfold, or God and sex." She interrogated the model, who had posed only to raise money for her college tuition, asking her about her sexual fantasies and whether she thought that posing nude would make nice Jewish boys reject her as a serious marriage possibility. The rabbi wanted to talk about the objectification of sex and its negative impact on genuine intimacy but was soon challenged by the audience for his highly publicized Jewish outreach efforts to television stars.

The moderator cared only about extracting lewd sexual details from anyone who was willing to share them. Once this proved impossible, she took a different tack, breaking a Jewish code of conduct by calling attention to the fact that the pinup model's father hadn't been born Jewish. Then she tried to get the girl to agree that Hugh Hefner was a destructive misogynist. For her part, the *Playboy* centerfold exhibited the most Jewish behavior of the evening. She refused to answer the question about her father's conversion, stating simply that she was "raised Jewish, and that's all that matters." And she was so upset by the invitation to speak ill of Hugh Hefner—the man who had paid her college tuition—behind his back that she began to cry. Little did she realize, she was the most actively Jewish person in

the room, having made a personal sacrifice to earn an education, defending the status of a convert, and refusing to
engage in backstabbing, the Jewish sin of *lashon hara.*

But these are not the elements of Judaism upon which
outreach marketers are determined to capitalize. They don't
mean to capitalize on Judaism at all, in fact; they're interested
in the Jews themselves. The object of the outreach game is to
get disaffected Jews to marry and then make more Jews. It
doesn't matter what the target market thinks Judaism actually
is, only that they identify themselves with the word. Once they
feel like Jews, they'll see the importance of defending Israel
and preserving the faith for future generations. Or so the logic,
and the demographic research, goes.

Instead of liberating Judaism from the cultural sinkhole in
which it has found itself, outreach efforts simply hope to dig
another, albeit hipper, one. Like all marketers, they communicate through intimidation. At their core, they are no different
from synagogues that appeal to desperate returnees, those that
twist the bonds of community to the needs of fund-raising,
those that put their heads in the sand by cloaking themselves in
the hues of Eastern European nostalgia, or those that distort
a religion based in literacy and iconoclasm into a magical
set of mysterious and impenetrable rituals. Instead of using
Judaism's built-in mechanisms for evolution and inviting
the Jewish community to take part in a daring reappraisal, they
wrap new layers around the religion they mean to preserve,

making it even less accessible to those who might be interested in bringing Judaism to the next level. They are turning the very best Jews away.

The most aggressive outreach groups don't mean to change Judaism or its packaging at all; instead they try to change the status of lapsed Jews by changing the way they think and altering what they believe. One Orthodox group, Aish HaTorah, has an indoctrination program that rivals the most sophisticated American cults in its use of persuasive techniques. They sponsor intensive learning trips to Israel, stage elaborate "awards ceremonies" in Jerusalem for wealthy Jewish American executives, and host Shabbat weekends for potential returnees at the homes of practicing Orthodox model families. A young former dot-com executive I know who went through the process told me that in spite of his efforts to view the entire experience satirically, he was nonetheless drawn in and "affected for months."

I myself was approached by the group and invited to a rabbi's home for Shabbat dinner. Meanwhile, from a seemingly unrelated branch of the organization, I was asked to contribute to their newsletter an essay I had published about Shabbat. The dinner was an outrageous spectacle, in which the rabbi's children were used to interview the guests about our views on Judaism and Israel. That tactic was interesting in that it prevented us from responding honestly to the obvious sales effort—these were only children, after all. Would they get in trouble if we didn't respond appropriately? Nevertheless, I reacted truthfully to the young boy's questions about the Holy Land, telling him I didn't much like our policies and that I found Israel to be more of an impediment than a spur to my own relationship to Judaism. Monday morning, I was informed by e-mail that my essay had been reviewed by Aish HaTorah's "higher authorities" and deemed unsuitable. Alas, to reach out successfully, such groups may have to learn to take in as well.

Whether Jewish organizations hope to increase the Jewish ranks by changing the hearts and minds of lapsed members or simply changing the outward trappings of Jewish institutions, their ultimate failure stems from their shared inability to address the problems underlying Judaism today. In fact, their methods exacerbate them. The text is not open for scrutiny; it is intentionally left closed. Sanctity is granted by priestly beings to the masses. Community is either forgone or leveraged in the name of fund-raising or a sexy come-hither.

Many rabbis and Jewish leaders understand that their tactics are contrary to the spirit of Judaism but believe that the pressing need for more bodies and wallets that can be tallied as Jewish outweighs the short-term damage caused by distorting the religion's theological and ethical foundations. But it does force us to ask who, really, is lapsing Judaism.

HOW WE GOT HERE

✡

Perhaps we shouldn't blame Judaism's misguided outreach operatives. Today's temples and philanthropies are merely continuing a trend that began over a century ago, as Jews wrestled with the combined impact of modernity, and modern prejudices, on Judaism.

It's not really the rabbis' fault that most prayer books no longer say what we mean. A typical Saturday morning worship service still includes a prayer that thanks God for not making us women, numerous references to being God's "chosen people," an understanding of famine as God's punishment for our misdeeds, and a prayer for God to resurrect the dead and bring us all to Israel. On Rosh Hashanah, we repeatedly recite that God is busy choosing who will live and who will die in the coming year. Who honestly wants to say things like this, particularly as one's most profound spiritual practice? This is why thoughtful Jews looking for a spiritual practice that reflects their innermost beliefs end up turning elsewhere or nowhere. Their honesty and integrity demand it.

How is Judaism to respond? The most liberal temples simply change the prayers to make them more palatable to modern audiences, which often leaves congregants feeling as though they are not practicing "authentic" Judaism. Moderate temples adopt new prayer books that leave the Hebrew as it is but change the English translations to hide the more retrograde sentiments. Congregants who happen to learn of the difference between the English and Hebrew sides of the page are left to deal with the cognitive dissonance on their own. The most Orthodox institutions leave the text exactly as it is and, instead, work to change their congregants' beliefs to match those voiced in their prayers. As a result, there are otherwise intelligent and educated Jews in America who nonetheless maintain the obsolete racist and sexist beliefs of our ancestors from centuries ago. In all of these cases, Judaism's evolution is either obscured or repressed.

Instead of engaging congregants in an honest reevaluation of Judaism in the context of our tradition of community-driven exchange, most synagogues take a hands-off approach to liturgy. These texts and prayers, though written by human beings no better than anyone else, are treated as sacred and inviolable texts. It's not solely the fault of Jewish leaders. Jewish laypeople have adopted an increasingly consumerist posture toward our experience of synagogue. Our rabbis are the professionals, charged with doing the right thing on our behalf. When we disagree with their choices, we simply take our business elsewhere. No mechanisms exist through which we can initiate a meaningful dialogue about our Jewishness.

How did we find ourselves in such a mess?

Modernity and misfortune. The rise of science and more advanced forms of literary criticism in the 1800s challenged cosmopolitan Jews, doggedly determined advocates of rationalism that they were, to reexamine their beliefs with an eye toward making them compatible with new discoveries. Meanwhile, the rise of new, scientifically justified forms of racism and persecution led Jews to alter their practices to make them appear less aberrant. Criticizing messianic fervor was one thing, becoming labeled as bloodthirsty Christ-killers with a genetic propensity for depravity was another. In spite of their efforts to fit in with their European contemporaries, Jews were singled out as targets in the most scientifically conceived extermination yet witnessed on earth. Efforts to understand why God would have permitted such atrocities led Jews to bend their religious convictions even further. These three forces combined to untether Judaism from its historically progressive moorings.

Although Jews of the sixteenth and seventeenth centuries embodied the spirit of the Enlightenment for its concern with human rights and emancipation, the eighteenth century brought an altogether new set of discoveries that forced them to question the divine authority of their most sacred texts and theistic doctrines.

The rise of rationalism rapidly changed Jews' understanding of their relationship to creation and the cosmos. Copernicus looked through his telescope and told human beings they were not at the center of the universe. Kant proved through logic that no one can see what is out there in reality. Darwin's observations of biology showed that people were not placed on earth as fully created humans, but evolved from sludge just like all the other animals. Freud's theories of psychology convinced people that they weren't even rational beings, but were directed by the chaotic whims of an unseen subconscious. How were Jews to reconcile their myth of creation and their divine place in God's great scheme with these new and seemingly antireligious conclusions? To modern rationalists, the notion of miracles had become preposterous.

Meanwhile, the Enlightenment's emphasis on individualism, though terrific for social justice, wreaked havoc on the authority of the core Jewish myths. The Old Testament, after all, is just that: a testament. Its first five books, which constitute the Torah, are to be accepted because they represent the testimony of the six hundred thousand who are purported to have witnessed the miracles on Mount Sinai. (Numerologists found further confirmation of this authority in the fact that the Torah can be understood as containing six hundred thousand characters, if you include the spaces.) From the Inquisition through the Enlightenment, faith in the Jewish doctrine was based on the authority of these eyewitnesses. But new focus on the experience of the individual led educated, thinking Jews to look for more personal and experiential justifications for their salvation and connection to divinity.

So while rationalist science negated the possibility of miracles, the emancipation of the individual diminished the authority of the forefathers' testament. Direct, critical, and academic analysis of the Torah rose in popularity, particularly in Germany, leading to the conclusion that books had been written by four main sets of authors or influences: the early Jahvist and Elohist schools, which refer to God as Jahweh and Elohanu, respectively; the Deuteronomist, whose revisionist book of Deuteronomy was added to consolidate the Israelites in the face of invasion; and the priestly, or legal, additions made after the Babylonian exile, which created rules for a more itinerant population. This critical analysis, supported by the concurrent discoveries of archaeologists and historians, showed that each thread was meant to push a different theological, cultural, or political agenda. By applying the techniques of literary criticism to the Torah, the nineteenth-century Germans had removed the "gray areas" that tended to lead worshipers to a more faith-based acceptance of the texts' divine origins, and their conclusions are widely accepted by academics to this day.

Their discoveries shouldn't have caused the shock that they did. Spinoza and other scholars had already concluded centuries earlier that the final draft of the Torah was spliced together by Ezra, a head scribe, after the return from exile, around 500 B.C.E. Even Ezra's contemporaries would have surely recognized that many of the Torah's stories were culled from other Near Eastern traditions and sometimes even quoted verbatim. Some passages, taken from Egyptian documents, were never fully translated into Hebrew. The covenant itself borrows its language from well-known war treaties. Very few in the educated elite should have believed that the Torah represented the unadulterated word of God, since the talmudists had already clearly identified many of the errors still remaining in the written text due to inaccuracies in its oral transmission.

Nonetheless, the factual evidence of the Torah's human origins shook the faithful, and new schools of religious philosophy had to be developed to accommodate the contradictions wrought by modernity. Why would people follow the laws of the Torah if they didn't believe they were from God himself? Philosophers like Gotthold Ephraim Lessing argued for believers to achieve "truths of reason" by turning to history and logic, while Kierkegaard proposed that a personal commitment to God could be achieved through a "leap of faith" over the chasm of evidence to the contrary. Later existentialists, like Martin Buber, rejected the divinity of *halakhah* altogether, while his friend Franz Rosenzweig proposed that the laws were developed quite spontaneously by human beings after their encounter with the divine. In any case, the shift in Judaism toward a new kind of secular humanism was under way. The differing reactions of Jews to this transformation of their religion led to the initial division of Jews between the Reform and Orthodox movements.

Most Jews were already looking for a change. After the short-lived emancipations they enjoyed following the French Revolution, the Jews of Europe were once again reviled and relegated to ghettos. German Jews felt that if only they could make themselves look and act more like regular Germans, they might be accepted as equals. The Reform movement sought to "normalize" Jewish ritual while emphasizing its modern strands. In its most progressive reform, the movement rewrote prayers that pleaded for the coming of the Messiah and the return to Israel to read more as odes to a spirit of brotherhood among all people. But they also rebuilt their synagogues as "temples," complete with arks and a stage, in order to make them appear more like the churches in which sacraments were performed. They introduced choral singing, translated prayers into German, and conducted new confirmation services for young people in the style of other Germanic houses of worship. Rabbis donned robes, stood behind pulpits, delivered sermons, and performed weddings in imitation of their Christian counterparts.

In a desire to fit in better with their xenophobic contemporaries, Jews adjusted their style of worship to conform to a more theatrical set of rituals designed originally for the Catholic mass. Jews ended up succumbing to a passive relationship to deity, without the comfort of a human-faced God like Jesus. They got the worst of both faiths and were left with an internally inconsistent religion.

Traditionally, the rabbis' main function was educational. They spoke to the congregation in the synagogue only twice a year, before Passover in order to remind Jews of specific rules and again before Yom Kippur to explain the meaning of repentance. Otherwise, their job was to teach Torah study in a classroom around a big table. Occasionally, their knowledge of Jewish law would enable them to resolve a local dispute. Religious services were led by the cantor, who stood at a table in the middle of the room, surrounded by congregants and other laypeople.

By changing the role of rabbi to that of a minister and putting him on what amounted to a stage in front of the room, reformers inadvertently led congregants to think about their own role in services very differently. Rabbis were now intermediaries between Jews and the God and laws with which they had always enjoyed personal relationships. Instead of focusing on the community of congregants with whom they were worshiping, Jews faced a stage and listened to the words of their rabbi, engaged in responsive reading, or followed along in rabbi-led rituals.

Congregants couldn't help but regress into a more child-like relationship to their rabbi and the religion he ministered. They transferred parental authority onto the rabbi and expected him to exemplify the piety to which they themselves could only strive. This served only to isolate rabbis from the spiritual communities on whom they could once depend for comfort and support.

Relieved of personal, adult responsibility for their religious practices, Jews tended to perform rituals and observances in a more perfunctory fashion. The religion became less participatory and more talismanic. Traditions like the mezuzah on the doorpost or a skullcap on one's head now served not as a point of mental focus, but as a hollow, rote performance or compulsive superstition. Religious education stressed how to behave, but very rarely delved into *why*.

The Orthodox movement rose in reaction to these reformations. Their yeshivas (religious schools) developed an ethos against the modernism they saw as the root of Judaism's disintegration. Taking a stance of staunch opposition to the spirit of autonomy and innovation sweeping Europe, the Orthodox separated themselves from the greater culture and resolved to believe that the oral and written law were of divine origin, no matter what the "evidence" to the contrary.

In reaction to the reformations occurring all around them, they resolved to take a different but equally huge leap backward. It was an unprecedented hunkering down in the face of what they saw as unbridled liberalism. The Torah and *halakhah* were to be understood not as the products of human inspiration and creativity, but as sacred transmissions from God. The job of Jews was but to preserve, protect, and perform these decrees. Though formulated as an alternative to Reform Judaism, orthodoxy also led its followers to regress into a more passive relationship to scripture. Orthodox Torah and Talmud study rejected the modern discipline of literary criticism, shunning questions of a text's origins or authorship in favor of simply ascertaining how it reflects God's will and how his laws still apply.

In spite of Jews' efforts to either imitate or insulate themselves from the practices of their neighbors, they were only to encounter new and scientifically justified forms of prejudice. One might expect that the ascendance of the scientific model and industrial culture would be accompanied by a corresponding rise in modern, cosmopolitan thinking. But Europeans reacted to the impact of modernity with the same fear and confusion as the Jews. The divine rights of nations and races were being threatened. Disconnected from their own ties to racial superiority, and disoriented by new questions of the legitimacy of their national origin, Europeans found in Jews a scapegoat for the questions posed by new sciences and technologies.

Ironically, they employed these very tools and methods in their persecution of the Jews. Although Freud had already (and quite correctly, we'll soon see) characterized Judaism as an idea rather than a specific race, his former student Carl Jung developed his own theories of a Jewish "racial memory" that accounted for their genetic propensity for destructive iconoclasm. The Nazi exterminations of Jews on the basis of sci-entifically rationalized "eugenics" research further engrained this false sense of ethnic identity. Although scientists know now that there is absolutely no genetic basis for race (aside from the genetic markers that come to characterize any people who are insulated for centuries), the Holocaust experience and other violent persecution throughout the twentieth century intensified the belief that Jews were a genetically unique and "chosen people." These assertions fueled Jews' paranoia, while exacerbating their conflicting self-images of ideological superiority and genetic inferiority. While the Jews came to believe that they were chosen alone, as a race, to enact God's will, the Nazis saw them as chosen for a different fate alto-gether. Thanks again to the efficiencies of modern science and engineering, the Nazis were able to enact their "final solution" with a mechanical precision and on a scale unimaginable before then.

The very biblical proportions of the Holocaust, combined with a more primitive understanding of the Torah itself, led to a conflation of Jewish myth with Jewish history. What the Nazis had done was so terrible, so inexplicable, that God must have been behind it. These events seemed to be occurring on a biblical scale. Parallels were drawn between having witnessed Auschwitz in the twentieth century and having witnessed the events on Mount Sinai. They were understood as part of the same continuum. But by choosing to view their history as biblical, Jews couldn't help but view their Bible as history. The concentration camps were true artifacts of literal history, so the events in the Torah began to be regarded as literal history, too.

People no longer understood the cataclysms of the Old Testament—from the plagues to the parting of the Red Sea—as metaphors for the birth of a new people. They were reduced to historical fact. Worse, to question the literal and historical validity of the Torah was equated, emotionally, with questioning the reality of the Holocaust and disrespecting the millions who were killed in Nazi gas chambers. Even this discussion of the Holocaust's impact on Jewish theology is somewhat disrespectful and premature, taking place as it does while so many people directly impacted by the Nazi atrocities are yet alive. Still, we have little alternative but to go on with the painstaking inquiry. For the stated mission of the Nazis was not simply to wipe out the Jewish people, but to end "the Jewish question." We must not allow them to succeed.

The fear of further reprisals confirmed the Jewish identity as a quest for survival against all odds, while limiting the definition of Judaism from a set of universal ideas to an indelible racial brand. Following the Holocaust, the establishment of the first Jewish nation in two thousand years grounded the notion of Israel in a physical piece of territory. Although Zionism was conceived long before World War II, Israel became widely regarded as a gift and recompense from the world for having endured the Shoah (annihilation). The

Jews' just reward for their supreme sacrifice. The Jewish enlightenment may have first separated the church and state, but Zionism put them back together again. Now, like other nations, the Jews had a flag under which to rally, a race with which to identify, and a country to protect. At the time, they had little reason to believe that this protectionism would one day reach near obsessive proportions and pose a real threat to the pluralist and universal values they had developed in the Diaspora.

But it did. By the 1950s, American Jewish education had devolved into the ethnocentric propaganda of Zionism and racial preservation. Jews' natural role as advocates of universal social justice and intellectual exchange degenerated to that of global watchdog. As they kept their ears to the ground for fear of persecution or worse, the Jewish tradition of prophecy and cultural design became one of survivalist future casting. The incessant Arab attacks presented Jews with a wealth of immediate, identifiable enemies. And these enemies were more feared than the decline of the most elemental and timeless Jewish ideals. Judaism's universal applications were surrendered to the seemingly pressing realities of state and race.

The intellectual tradition of European Judaism was frowned upon by Zionists and other ardent Jewish protectors. New York radical Meir Kahane, founder of the Jewish Defense League, berated "yeshiva boys" for their passivity and encouraged a more macho, warlike posture for his people.

He organized night patrols in Brooklyn to protect *Yiddishe bubbes* from black youth, and he launched campaigns to send money and weapons to Israel. The Jewish biblical word for inner spiritual strength—*uzi*—became the brand name for an Israeli-made machine gun.

Discussions at synagogues concentrated less on spirituality than on fund-raising for a besieged Israel and stemming the threat intermarriage posed to Jewish racial purity. To young American Jews like me, who had no direct experience of the persecution that our elders suffered, temple became a drag. It was a place where we were told of our great obligation to preserve and protect our special, chosen people against a slew of encroaching dangers—military, genetic, and cultural. But what was in it for *us*?

The most enlightened Jewish leaders worked simply to come up with more interesting ways to instill the same values of Zionism and continuity. They organized trips to Israeli kibbutzim, where young people could be exposed directly to the utopian nationalistic ideals of the Jewish nation. Others created summer camps and weekend excursions to the country, where children were supervised by young, hip, pot-smoking Jewish college students. Sex, drugs, and Zionist programming.

But racial identification has a correspondingly negative effect on a people's self-image. This was especially so in the newly built suburbs of midcentury United States, where prosperity and happiness were measured by the ability to cast off one's European affectations and adopt the values of the American dream. To Jews in particular, with centuries of less friendly immigration experiences, America was not a melting pot at all, but a preexisting Anglo-Saxon culture with which they would have to conform in order to succeed. As soon as they were able, Jews purchased icons such as Cadillacs, joined "restricted" country clubs, and resorted to plastic surgery as a way of fitting in with a people whom they regarded as "other," even superior. Formerly spiritual experiences like the bar mitzvah were reduced, in the modern social schema, to an assumption of upper-middle-class American values—the Jewish version of a debutante ball. More energy was spent on catering a bar mitzvah afterparty than studying the Torah portion.

Any doubts about having dropped the real torch of Judaism were soothed by the belief that somewhere—maybe in Brooklyn or Jerusalem—some genuine Orthodox Jews were preserving the faith for generations to come. Reform Jews understood that they were practicing "Judaism light" and turned over authority of the religion and Israel to extremists. Secular Jews found themselves agreeing inwardly as their Orthodox counterparts called them "lapsed." They'd make up for it by sending another check to a worthy Zionist cause or showing up once a year at the High Holidays to atone. Just keeping one's children marrying within the faith was victory enough. By the time moderate Jews realized just how far they had relinquished control over their religion and Holy Land to Judaism's own version of fundamentalists, it was too late. We'd rather switch than fight.

Most of us were so turned off by our culture, our practice, and the policies of our namesake nation that we left Judaism shortly after our bar mitzvahs. It just wasn't cool, and it didn't jibe with our politics. Our religious education, such as it was, ended at the age of thirteen. By the 1970s, college-age Jews were turning en masse to Buddhism and other Eastern spiritual systems that more directly answered our desire for an experience of the transcendent. We turned to science, social activism, even yoga, to engage with sensibilities that are, in a sense, more Jewish, yet we were labeled "lapsed" and mourned as our people's failures.

Those who did remain in the fold tended to believe that the supreme role of good Jews was to protect Judaism itself. The temple to which one belonged wasn't simply a place to pray—it was now a sacred space in its own right. Judaism was not a set of ideas to be shared, but a religion to be protected from the decadent influence of secular humanism and the hostile actions of anti-Semites. The kosher laws were not a way to insure the ethical treatment of animals, but a way to insulate oneself from the unsanitary habits of the common "goy." Instead of serving as a way to share insights with others, con-version was forced on prospective non-Jewish mates as an ultimatum, treating them like members of a lower species who require domestication before they can be considered suitable parents for Jewish children.

As the religion and its institutions got increasingly closed-minded and self-interested, fewer and fewer people felt any reason to stay Jewish at all. And so the outreach efforts commenced.

It's no wonder Judaism has found itself in a dilemma.

REVIVING JACOB

Fear of persecution, combined with a new, simplistic relationship to the Jewish texts has undermined Judaism's more time-honored traditions of inquiry and iconoclasm. New interpretations of Torah, or the suggestion that its stories are anything but factual history, are shunned as an unnecessary "watering down" of Jewish holiness or an invitation for continued persecution by outsiders looking for any excuse to cast doubt on the Jewish claim of being the "chosen." It undermines the credibility of the Jewish narrative and Jewish suffering—from the mythical slavery in Egypt to the very real gas chambers of Auschwitz. If it's not "good for the Jews," then it is not to be discussed. No, the Jewish religion is to be set in stone, even though it was invented to resist just such a fate.

This is how Jews lost the plot of our own story—the one we

were writing together. The institutions we created to protect our best insights ended up suffocating them. Our texts and practices still hold the keys to an extraordinarily progressive and satisfying spiritual path for those who wish to be both smart *and* good. But our insistence on maintaining their divine authority and selling them without discussion to our "lapsed" constituency robs them of their true force and meaning.

Finally, by appointing our most extremely Orthodox members as the caretakers of religious doctrine, we disempower ourselves from being able to do anything about our misgivings. The religion seems to get more racist, patriarchal, parochial, and homophobic rather than less. Young adults raised in this tradition find that their own painstakingly realized life choices—from sexuality to intermarriage—lead them to be shunned by their own religious community. Like recovering cult members, they find themselves longing for the false security of unilateral decree yet unable to reconcile their passively learned faith with their actively earned social development. There is no room for negotiation.

Today, most Jews no longer identify our religion with the iconoclasm, abstract monotheism, or universal social justice at its core. Judaism is experienced as more of an obligation, even an albatross. By repressing the transparency of our texts, diminishing the egalitarian and participatory quality of our evolving theology, and underestimating our community's ability to respond more creatively to the challenge of assimilation, we have reduced Judaism from a deconstructing, demystifying, and do-it-yourself spiritual path to a closed book. We have succumbed to our own form of fundamentalism.

Where is Jacob? Who is still wrestling with God?

Now, perhaps more than ever, the world needs the gifts that the world's first pan-cultural, globally conscious religion has to offer. The spiritual thirst is there. So is the hunger for the kinds of open, participatory, and intelligent discourse that made Jewish institutions famous in the past.

But before we can do Judaism to the world, we had better do Judaism to itself.

Three

A RENAISSANCE
TRADITION

THE GOOD NEWS IS THAT Judaism has faced such crises before and survived. In each instance, a small minority of the Jewish population adopted a radically recontextualized understanding of the religion's fundamental tenets. And in every instance, only that small minority flourished, carrying into the next era what would from then on be called "Judaism."

Each successful shift involved experiencing, or reexperiencing, Judaism's most essential insights of iconoclasm, basic humanism, and the abstractness of God in a new way. Indeed, the mandate for radical reappraisal might be one of Judaism's most enduring traditions—and the source of its unparalleled endurance. Judaism itself was developed through the reinvention of pagan beliefs in the new light of social justice. Rituals that involved human sacrifice or idolatry were reworked to acknowledge higher-minded ideals than assuaging God's wrath or guaranteeing a good harvest. The pagan quarter-moon festival, as we have seen, was reborn in its new context as the Sabbath—a labor holiday dedicated to the contemplation of the sanctity of life.

Radical reinvention was not merely Judaism's birthright, but the ongoing and defining character of the Jewish experiment. It is a way of maintaining continuity with the past while allowing for a faith to evolve into the future. Judaism does not change merely to stay with the times. It has been built to change and to cause change.

Indeed, the paramount Jewish tradition is to question and break with tradition itself. But Judaism does so less through revolution than renaissance—literally, the rebirth of old ideas in a new context. Reorientations. That's why Judaism's greatest leaps forward always occur during moments like these—when Jews feel they have lost the plot. For it is only then that Jews are motivated to reach back into their core beliefs and time-tested techniques and reinterpret them for a new reality.

TO LIFE

Take the Israelites' very first leap of this kind—their emergence from Egypt. Here was a people for whom pantheism had proven disastrous. The worship of animal gods and the building of temples to death cults meant that human life could be devalued more easily. This society institutionalized many forms of indentured servitude, even slavery. This is because in the pre-Judaic era, rife with child sacrifice and the worship of monuments to the dead, human life itself was not cherished.

The Exodus story is understood by most historians (but, alas, not by most practicing Jews) as the mythological birth of the Jewish people—a group of foreign workers living in the city of Goshen who would create a new society no longer based on monuments, physically realized character gods, or the sacrifice of the living to the dead or iconic. These workers were not Jews yet at all, but essentially Egyptian.

The plagues their new "God" manifested were not simply a way of insuring the Israelites' escape from their captors. An all-powerful God could have taken care of that much more efficiently. The elaborate plagues represented the destruction of the gods and icons that these resident workers themselves would need to betray in order to accept this new life-affirming deity and the more universal concept of sanctity he offered. As we have seen, each of the plagues actually symbolizes the desecration of an Egyptian deity by the Israelites' God. Ultimately, the Israelites themselves sacrificed a lamb and put the blood on their doors. This offering would have been well understood as a blaspheming of the Egyptians' most sacred god, the ram-headed Khnum, creator of the universe.

In the mythical Bible story, this sacrifice—literally the surrender of an Egyptian god that many Israelites probably worshiped themselves at the time—caused their homes to be "passed over" when the angel of death came to kill all the Egyptian firstborn sons. Of course, such myths weren't taken literally until very recently. People of the period would have understood this symbolism as easily as we understand the satires on late-night television. And in its intended metaphoric context, the allegory becomes quite clear: The Jews had evolved beyond Egypt, the firstborn civilization, as well as their own pagan practice of sacrificing firstborn sons.

They were now the self-proclaimed descendants of the mythic patriarch Abraham, the first man to be approached by a new, abstract God who did not demand child sacrifice. No, just a little piece of foreskin and a few goats killed at regular intervals were enough to satisfy this kinder, gentler God's lust for flesh. The covenant, first made with Abraham but, ultimately, confirmed with the entire Jewish people at Mount Sinai, was to smash all idols, end human sacrifice, and promote social justice. Indeed, the first thing these former slaves gave themselves was a work holiday: Sabbath.

It should not surprise us that Judaism was born, in part, out of a labor resistance movement. Its creators understood that idol worship devalues humanity and compromises social justice. By adopting a more abstract deity, and a more interior way of resonating with him, the Jews hoped to develop a society based in autonomous and thoughtful living rather than mindless slavery and death. The Jews were "chosen" by God—or, more accurately, they chose themselves—to promote these values around the world.

This leap forward in theology and ethics did not mark a terrifying discontinuity for humanity, however much we'd like to believe the Jews invented something entirely new. No, it was simply a recontextualization of ancient rites in a new context. A renaissance. The sacrifice of the child was reinvented through the sacrifice of animals. The pagan quarter-moon festival was reborn as Sabbath. The worship of a lamb was reworked into Pesach, or Passover. The idols of pagan gods were replaced by the conspicuously icon-free Ark of the Covenant.

These revised practices and beliefs addressed the same human emotions and frailty but redirected them toward a new and more ethically evolved set of values. The death cults of Egypt and pagan sacrificial rites of Canaan were reinvented through the life-affirming values of early Judaism. The Israelites still needed the reassurance that a good sacrificial ritual provided, so they retained the priests and temples of their forebears. They still depended on the whims of nature to provide for a bountiful crop, so they kept their major holy days on the harvest schedule. But they invented new forms for these institutions and celebrations that affirmed the sanctity of human life and the necessity of an ethical code to insure the rights of everyone.

While Egyptian priests' primary function was to administer

death rites and maintain the tombs, Israelite priests, descendants of Aaron's tribe of the *cohanim,* were strictly forbidden to touch the dead. In a complete reversal of their prerenaissance function, the *cohanim's* ritual purity was defined by their insulation from all things having to do with death. The *cohanim* were the same old priests, dressed in the same robes and working in the same sorts of temples, but reborn in a completely new context—that of life.

Holidays were adapted to a new life-affirming context as well. By reframing pagan harvest rituals as celebrations of various moments in the Exodus saga, Jews could bring themselves to appreciate the Torah as God's ultimate gift to his people. Sukkot, or the Feast of the Tabernacles, is a reinterpretation of the grape and olive harvest, in which Jews dine in small structures to commemorate God's protection during the Israelites' forty years in the desert. Although early Jews still brought barley to the Temple for Shavuot celebrations in thanks for the harvest, the holiday was redefined as a tribute to God for handing down the Torah through Moses at Mount Sinai. It is not simply his supply of grain, but God's ethical template that sustains the Jews as a people.

By redefining their traditional practices in the new context of Judaism, early Jews gave themselves the tools and inspiration to evolve a more enlightened set of sensibilities. The Holy Temple, though bloodlustfully pagan when viewed through a modern lens, nonetheless redefined the very purpose of sacrifice from a preparation for death to a confirmation of the value of human life. The word *chai,* meaning "life," emerged as the fundamental tenet of the Israelites as they exorcised themselves of their own susceptibility to idol worship and the injustices implicit in an idolatrous society. As a result, the Jewish Bible doesn't explore the death and possible afterlife of the individual except in one short passage. On numerous occasions, though, the text makes it clear that death is not to be valued. One psalmist (Psalm 115) writes, "The dead cannot praise the Lord, nor any who go down into silence. But we will bless the Lord now and forever." Likewise, in Deuteronomy we are passionately advised to "choose life." Such admonitions were meant for a people still struggling with the lure of the death cults from which they came.

Even the famous Jewish toast *L'chaim,* "To life," finds its roots in the victory cry of a people who have escaped a civilization based in death. It's almost naughty in its replacement of the solemnity of death and the afterlife with the celebration of the here and now.

Likewise, replacing the sanctity of the harvest with that of the Torah put an unprecedented emphasis on the laws through which people interacted with one another, instead of the rites they used to coerce their gods into providing for them. Holidays based in the historical or mythic birth of the "people of the book" marked the first stage of God's recession from the affairs of men. It helped launch the inquiry into abstract monotheism and its many implications, by forcing people to relate not to the rain or the soil as proof of God's benevolence, but to his prescriptions for human behavior. The Jewish God still made demands of his people, but these demands were now no longer directed toward his own deification. God's commands were reborn in the context of ethics and social justice.

Although tracing Judaism back to its roots in paganism might shake the foundations of fundamentalists who need to affirm God's direct authorship of everything Jewish, acknowledging the process through which the first Jewish renaissance recontextualized the pagan into the profoundly humanistic is critical to our purpose. It serves as the first and foremost precedent to the process we must undergo today. History shows us that Judaism was not born of itself, bootstrapped and independent of all that went before, but was rather a rebirth of old ideas in a new context. This is a noble origin, not to be ignored or suppressed as many rabbis and fundamentalists attempt to do today, but used to support us in our own resolve to enact a renaissance of our own.

INTO METAPHOR

It was almost a thousand years before Jews were required to undergo such a radical shift in their understanding of the sacred, again inspired by oppressive external forces— this time real ones. The Israelites had settled in Canaan by around 1100 B.C.E., established their kingdom, and built their Temple. Still, they were under constant threat from expansionist neighbors in the north. Over the next twelve centuries, the Assyrians, Babylonians, Greeks, and finally the Romans conquered part or all of Israel.

Each time they were vanquished or exiled, former Judeans were compelled to reevaluate their connection to God and Israel. If they were God's chosen, why had he forsaken them? And how would they show their devotion—and avoid his wrath—if they could no longer sacrifice animals at the Holy Temple?

It was a push-and-pull process that spanned several centuries, beginning with the warnings of the prophets in the eighth century B.C.E. and ending around the time of Christ, with the final Roman destruction of the Second Temple. At each stage of increasing threat, no one was exactly sure whether to retreat into a more concretized faith or press ahead into the seeming uncertainty of abstract and personally experienced devotion.

It began with retreat. After the Israelites' Northern Kingdom was vanquished by the Assyrians in 722 B.C.E., King Josiah of Judea feared his Southern Kingdom might be next. He realized that in the three hundred years since Israel was established, many Jews had reverted to their ancient, Canaanite ways. They were worshiping bulls, conducting sex rites, and even, according to some evidence, sacrificing firstborn children again. Whether their polytheistic practices were actually as devolved as Josiah suspected or merely a healthy resurgence of a goddess sensibility is left for historians to decide. Racked with fear about the frailty of the remaining kingdom, and concerned that the impending Assyrian invasion was a sign of his people's denial of their protecting God, Yahweh, Josiah attempted to reinforce what he saw as traditional Judaism.

This is when the book of Deuteronomy was "discovered," complete with its unequivocal demand that the Israelites worship Yahweh "alone" and "with all your heart, and all your might." Deuteronomy reiterates most pointedly the commands from God to tear down the altars, wipe out the Canaanites, and not deal or, worse, mate with native inhabitants. Josiah's reformation of Judaism was designed to convince the Israelites, in no uncertain terms, that it was their birthright and their duty to claim and protect the Promised Land. This is when the Jews were elevated to the status of God's chosen people: "It is you that *Yahweh* our *elohim* has chosen to be his very own people out of all the peoples of the earth." If nothing else, it prepared his soldiers for holy battle.

The prophets simultaneously developed a more sophisticated articulation of the Jewish ideals they saw eroding through an emphasis on ritualistic worship. Because the Israelites' rites were based on those of their Canaanite and Egyptian predecessors, there was a natural tendency for them to revert to their original idolatrous functions—especially when they were carried out with waning knowledge of their symbolism, or what distinguished them from pagan rites in the first place. Even though they gave Jews the chance to demonstrate devotion to Yahweh, the "right" God, these rituals meant nothing by themselves. They were metaphors. The prophets were at pains to show the Israelites that hollow worship only gave "lip service" to God. Temple rites and demonstrative fasts were no substitute for good actions and holy deeds. These could be carried out only in real life.

As the Southern Kingdom eventually fell to the Babylonians, the wealthy and educated classes—deemed capable of fomenting a revolution—were deported. Most of those who were left behind either reverted to Canaanite practices or retreated into highly insulated and literal-minded Jewish cults. Those who were exiled to Babylonia ended up taking the words of the prophets to heart and managed to develop the beginnings of a new kind of Judaism, based more in prayer and an internalized religious sensibility than in the outward manifestations of worship afforded by the Temple. By the time they returned to Israel in 522, they had the Torah with them and instituted reading and discussion.

Under the more benevolent rule of the Persians, the Jews rebuilt the Temple and performed sacrifices again, but other prayers, blessings, and rituals were now being integrated into the service. The sages (proto-rabbis, really) set these commandments to paper for Jews to carry God's word into everyday life instead of relegating to the Temple all that is holy.

These measures all helped to prepare the Jews for their devastating loss of Israel to the Romans in 70 C.E. and the final destruction of the Holy Temple. But not everyone was willing to stick with Judaism through such a catastrophe.

Many Jews who had been part of the messianic revolts turned to Christianity for its "new" testament to God. Like many radical Zionists today, who rely on the promise of a messianic age, the Jewish followers of Christ saw in his zeal the fighting spirit they would need to foist an insurrection. His image, unlike that of an abstract deity, gave them a human face to turn to in their despair and a human leader—though dead—behind whom to rally. Others were convinced that because the Roman gods had been victorious over Yahweh, this new pantheon now deserved their devotion. Still other Jews struggled in vain to recapture their independence and rebuild the Temple. But none of these efforts ultimately carried Judaism into the first millennium.

In fact, only the small minority of rabbis who realized that Judaism would have to become a "road show" were capable of reimagining and repackaging the religion for an era of Diaspora. Basing their theology on the words of the prophets, these rabbis concluded that the loss of the Temple and the ability to conduct sacred rites marked a leap forward in the holy covenant between Jews and their Lord. Without his physically realized and sacred Temple, God would no longer enter into the affairs of men. Instead, it was now a human responsibility to enact the holy teachings.

Many of these rabbis, especially the Pharisees, had been challenging the authority of the Temple priests for decades, arguing that the law, study, and prayer were more important than sacrificial rites. Recognizing the need for a form of intelligent worship and religious participation that didn't depend on a temple, they developed and maintained the oral law—a set of ideas about human behavior that were informed by the Torah but transmitted orally for centuries. These heady commentaries had been rejected by the more literal orders of the Jewish priesthood but now stood the best chance of bringing Judaism into an era with no kingdom or Temple.

As Jews continued to revolt against the Romans, however, an increasing number of rabbis were being killed. Who would be left to transmit the entirety of the oral law? So around 200 C.E. it was decided to record the oral law on paper, and these writings became the first books of the Talmud. Its intricate, intertextual wrapping of commentary around commentary was meant to re-create the inner corridors and chambers of the Temple, in literary form. The book's structure and function became a metaphor for the Holy Temple. The oldest of Jewish teachings could be reborn in the new context of sacred literature. This was not a crisis, but an opportunity to bring spirit into the mind and heart.

In order to seize upon this renaissance, Jews would have to become not less Jewish, but more so. Iconoclasm had to be applied not just to the beliefs of others, but to the Jews' own obsolete institutions. Humanism could no longer be taken for granted as a tenet, but had to be enacted on both a spiritual plane and in the affairs of men. And God, who had at least been symbolically accessible through the Temple rites, would have to be experienced through an even more abstract form of worship.

The rabbis packed up their Torahs and Talmuds and took them along into Greco-Roman culture, adapting Judaism to focus on the text. Study itself became the ultimate mitzvah, or blessing, and fit in well with the logic and knowledge-based values of secular Hellenist society. By transforming the synagogue into a house of study (*beit midrash*), the Jews succeeded in developing the first public education system for adults. But this new emphasis on insight and understanding also called for a more intimate and participatory relationship of the Jews with their abstract and unseen God.

God was no longer manifest in the Temple but was embodied by human beings in the synagogue. Each segment of the synagogue service corresponded to a different sacrificial rite in the Temple tradition. These parts of the service are still enacted in daily Jewish worship (the *musaf*—extra—prayer being the most awkward appendage of this one-for-one correspondence). The sacrifice itself was replaced by the reading of the Torah—a liturgical revision that outraged many incumbent Jewish leaders, who felt the text was too sacred for analysis and consideration by anyone but the priestly class. But this new movement, called "rabbinic Judaism," would prevail.

The rabbis had enough foresight and experience to predict that the exiled Jews, living among polytheistic people with more literal notions of God, might revert to a more idolatrous understanding of their own God. This is why they eventually decided to replace all textual references to "Yahweh" with the abbreviation of *yud hay, vuv hay,* which were themselves eventually replaced in prayer books with an even more abbreviated set of *yuds* that look almost like quotation marks. It's not much of a stretch to imagine what it felt like to read those abbreviations whenever one was supposed to infer the word *God.* It was as if to put one's fingers up in little quote signs while saying "God," fully cognizant that there was no such real thing—at least not as he could be understood. The glyphs just hold open the space.

If Temple Judaism was a literal performance of the Torah's rites, rabbinic Judaism was a metaphoric appreciation of their importance. Overwhelming evidence suggests that Jews did not understand the Torah literally, but saw in its mythology an allegory to their own experience of defeat and Diaspora. They may very well have seen their God not as a real entity, like the gods of the people among whom they lived, but as a metaphor, too.

The rabbis certainly understood that Jewish rituals do not serve God, whatever he may be. They serve humans in their effort to embody and enact a more God-like, or at least God-approved, way of living. The rabbinic renaissance transformed Judaism from a literal transposition of pagan practices into a metaphoric appreciation for the core values that God symbolizes. The stories and metaphors of Judaism are merely media—virtual containers for the sacred, which has no actual form.

THE CRISIS OF MODERNITY

But a virtual religion is as hard to practice as a virtual people are to hold together. Eventually, even the metaphors people use to represent a "real thing" come to be regarded as real things themselves, especially when people need something more tangible than a metaphor to hold on to in the face of annihilation.

Over the past few thousand years, and increasingly in the last century, the study and rituals designed to encourage an internalized, intimate relationship with God have themselves become calcified. It's no great wonder why. Without a sturdy institution to bind them to one another or to preserve their most sacred beliefs, European Jews from the fourteenth to the twentieth centuries came to value continuity over experience. The chief objective of Judaism became to preserve Judaism itself. Each new instance of widespread persecution convinced the Jews to retract from their promotion of science and modernity and retreat even further into the protective shell of social and cultural isolation. It's as if Jews' promotion of science, labor rights, and social evolution ends up costing them, in the end, whenever a tyrant means to base his power on the subjugation of his people.

The Inquisition and subsequent expulsion of the Jews from many of Europe's cultural centers repeatedly fractured them into retrograde, mystically inclined enclaves who prayed in futility for the Messiah. Holland was a notable exception, as persecution against Jews abated there through most of the sixteenth century. Several quite progressive Dutch Jewish philosophers emerged, who envisioned more just societal principles, including the separation of church and state, as the best remedies for their counterparts' woes in the rest of Europe. But no sooner could such a renaissance or enlightenment be imagined than its founders were subjected to another of the second millennium's many horrific anti-Semitic cleansings. Jews fought for the republics of eighteenth-century Europe and enjoyed momentary freedoms only to be relegated to the ghettos again once those republics were fully established. Neither did the Russian Revolution, again conceived in large part by Jews who were accepted at first as comrades, lead to any lasting equality for the Jewish people once the new regime was in place.

The catastrophic proportions of the Nazi Holocaust, following yet another of the Jews' seeming acceptances into European society, led them once again to question the motives of their withdrawn deity as well as their own strategy of integration. Like the Jews of the Roman period who attempted to rebuild the Temple, survivors and witnesses of the death camps concluded that they had just experienced an event of biblical proportions, willed by an angry God. And it has changed their relationship to Torah to this day. Now that the metaphoric value of the Jewish myths and rituals had been collapsed into history and superstition, their ability to serve as the triggers for intellectual inquiry was neutralized.

Progressive intellectualism, which had once been the Jews' calling card, was now equated with the modernist, assimilated European values that had cost Jews their six million lives. The work of philosophers like Martin Buber and, worse, some post-Holocaust existentialists had led Jews to question the "true" authority of their own teachings. By turning to philosophy instead of the Lord God, they felt they had mired themselves in relativism, ontology, and thought systems utterly incapable of addressing the great human despair they were now facing. They wanted their religion back. And back they went.

Most Jews attempted, in one way or another, to rebuild the Temple. Some turned to religious Zionism for its promise of messianic redemption once Israel is fully secured. Others sanctified the synagogue, turning local "temples" into the centerpieces of Jewish life and fund-raising. These were not—and still are not—places for study and discussion, but sanctuaries for worship. Unable to rationalize a Jewish relationship with God that could include the horror story of Nazi Germany, they retreated to a religion based in blind faith, embodied more in ritual than in active thought.

Those who clung to the scientific, intellectual, and philosophical advances of the modern era found themselves increasingly disenfranchised by religious institutions that encouraged unquestioning support of Israel, taught faith-based doctrine, and shunned the impulse for progressive idealism and universal values. The intellectuals enjoyed a more internalized Jewish sensibility and were not threatened by modernism at all. If anything, they were one of the prime motivating forces behind the modernist inquiry. The anti-authoritarian impulse of the modern era, complete with its reevaluation of nation-state, race, economics, and existence itself, was to them an affirmation, not a negation, of Judaism's core values of abstract monotheism, iconoclasm, and social justice. This is why so many of modernism's great thinkers were themselves Jews. The only values they meant to negate were those born of institutional lethargy or consensus denial or that found their authority in authority itself.

So a great split arose between secular, scientific Jews and more unquestioningly observant ones. Today, the most radically Orthodox Jews in America are not even permitted to attend secular schools. They cannot become doctors, lawyers, or philosophers and cannot participate in academic or scientific conversations. This is why they work in camera shops or the diamond district. Even observant members of Reform and Conservative communities tend to practice their faith with their heads in the sand, using synagogue as a spiritual safe haven from the many paradoxes of modern living. Meanwhile, most Jews who have pursued the sciences or cultural studies have felt the need to abandon religious institutions that increasingly negate the evidence to be observed in the real world. Without any connection to their religious tradition, however, they lose access to the spiritual dimensions of their disciplines and their lives.

This situation should sound familiar. Like the Israelites of the desert and the Jews of the exile, today's Jews are a fractured people in need of renaissance. Is it so very presumptuous to suggest that we might spearhead a discussion that launches a new set of inquiries into and expressions of what it means to be Jewish today? It's the way we've always launched renaissances, after all. Though it is with great reluctance that we assume this mantle, we—the literate, intelligent, and somewhat lapsed Jews of today—are as likely candidates as any to reinvent the practice of Judaism, on our own terms, together. The best hints we have of Judaism's potential for a future might be found within our own questions about the role of religion in our lives, the real downside, if any, of inter-marriage, our relationship with Israel, our obligation to our forefathers. These are the unresolved conflicts, ambivalences, and paradoxes churning within us that rarely reach the light of day—and they may actually bear fruit if we feed them rather than deny them.

For however much Judaism may serve as the source of our core beliefs, it is also the source of many misgivings. You are not the only one who sees great hypocrisy in the way modern Judaism relates to the rest of the world. Jewish institutions encourage us to "marry Jewish"—even going so far as to fund elaborate singles' social centers—but don't do very much to justify this strategy of continuity through what appears, to con-temporary sensibilities, anyway, as racism. Most of us still find ourselves inwardly hoping to find a Jewish mate, but we are uncertain as to our own motivations and from whence they originate. And whether they're progressive or racist.

Similarly, even the most "lapsed" of us tend to feel a cer-tain obligation to defend the Jewish homeland but find it hard to openly support a nation that engages in militaristic and pro-vocative policies. Does being Jewish require justifying aggressive West Bank settlers? And how can progressive, thinking Americans practice a religion that, in its most vocal expressions, still succumbs to homophobia and sexism? Can we simply remain silent during prayers that seem to espouse chauvinism or worse? And how can an enlightened individual sign on to a set of cultural values that are plagued by bourgeois aspirations and, dare we admit it, quite ostentatious materialism?

In short, how can we belong to a religion that is so hopelessly entrenched—or at least associated—with values we abhor, especially when we don't feel we are in any position to change it?

For these reasons and more, many of us have taken long, effortful journeys away from what we thought of as Judaism. Some of us became quite successful and respected in our secular endeavors, only to realize with painstaking clarity that the many insights and values we have come to fight for find their very foundations in the Jewish tradition we abandoned. Strangely, the very same culture from which we rebel also informs some of our most cherished beliefs. We come full circle.

Rather than denying this paradox, the way to move forward might be to embrace it. Tap it for the voltage within. Many of us experience Judaism as both a precious set of truths and a tiresome set of cultural baggage. But by engaging with this troublesome dynamic, we empower ourselves to explode our conflicting perceptions into altogether new forms. And in doing so, we can discover something about Judaism itself.

What if we were to apply the iconoclastic, uncompromising, and relentlessly inquisitive spirit of the stiff-necked people on ourselves and our beliefs? We would be doing Judaism *to* Judaism. It might not be easy. Judaism is a process in which no stone is left unturned—at least not for lack of willingness to question. And such an inquiry could not be taken lightly. In order to reengineer a religion, we will have to know it forward and backward. It's not a matter of just picking and choosing what we like and cavalierly discarding the rest. We would have to look at the whole thing and educate ourselves enough to be able to do so with some intelligence and perspective. Are we ready to embark on such a path?

We may have to be. These are the stress points on the Jewish model, the faulty hinges and joints that can no longer move in the direction we are attempting to take it. By asking the hardest questions of one another and ourselves in the light of day, we will expose what needs to be altered, what needs to be discarded, and what needs to be invented from scratch.

RENAISSANCE NOW

By permitting itself to undergo a renaissance of the same magnitude as the leap from paganism to monotheism, or Temple rituals to synagogue worship, Judaism can once again serve as an ethical, intellectual, and spiritual template for a civilization facing the challenges of globalization. It would be a struggle, but it would be worth it. In fact, a full-scale renaissance may be this religion's only hope for genuinely meaningful survival.

What is renaissance, exactly? It's a dimensional leap. Think of all those great Renaissance innovations we were taught in grammar school: perspective painting, calculus, circumnavigating the globe, the sonnet, and the printing press, to name just a few. What do all these features of the original Renaissance have in common? In one way or another, they all involve seeing three dimensions where there had previously been only two. Perspective painting allowed artists to depict three dimensions on a two-dimensional canvas. Calculus allowed mathematicians to describe curves and spheres using the arithmetic language of straight lines. Circular shipping routes changed our model of the world from a flat map to a round globe. The sonnet was the first form of poetry that explored the use of extended metaphors, ultimately in order to create the possibility for multiple, simultaneous perspectives on the same poem. The Gutenberg press broke the elites' monopoly on information and literacy, acknowledging more than one point of view on a given piece of text and permitting intellectual, social, and religious movements to rise up from the masses for the first time. The Renaissance moved many arts and disciplines from a flat literalness to a more dimensionalized, metaphoric understanding and expression.

Today, we are undergoing a similar shift—one that might

even be considered a renaissance all its own. Recent advances in science, technology, and thought such as the holograph, the fractal, chaos math, the Gaia hypothesis, and the Internet all intimate another leap in dimensional perspective. These late-twentieth-century innovations all suggest a new relationship between the individual and the whole. Scientists, mathematicians, and sociologists alike are reckoning with the possibility that each part of a network, in some small way, reflects the nature of the entire system.

The Gaia hypothesis holds that the Earth's ecosystem has maintained a regulated environment and climate for too long to be considered the result of climatic coincidence. The planet may more accurately be understood as a single, networked entity, using its many species of plant life and animals—including us— to maintain the health of the whole. Likewise, the Internet has changed our relationship to media as much as, if not more than, the Gutenberg press. Instead of simply being able to access the same information as the formerly literate classes, now we can all create and disseminate information of our own. Each computer terminal is a node in a network, and each user is a potential broadcaster. Finally, as anyone who has studied fractals, systems theory, or holography can tell you, an entire system—such as the weather or a human brain—is reflected, or recapitulated, in each of its parts. These new mathematics and technologies exploit nonlinear equations for their ability to re-create the self-similar properties of natural systems more accurately than the calculus equations of our previous renaissance. And what they suggest about our natural universe is that each part, in some small way, reflects the whole.

This emerging understanding of dimensionality might best be called "recapitulation." Each component recapitulates the entire system. It's a new, multidimensional perspective— and, to many, a frightening one.

For renaissances are tricky moments. They are periods when, thanks to the experience of a sudden shift in perspective, everything seems to be up for grabs. Authority is questioned. In the moment of reorientation, a struggle is waged among many different people and forces. The new maps that we draw and the updated models we build will all depend on who gains leverage during our collective negotiation.

Think of a renaissance as if it were like learning to play a video game. A boy buys a new game cartridge, reads the instruction booklet, and then embarks on his quest to kill aliens. He can play this way for hours, remaining within the confines of the game world. Eventually, however, he may decide to go out onto the Internet and join a discussion group about the game. There, he can learn the "cheat codes" for the game that allow him to access special features like extra weapons or increased energy levels. When he returns to the game with his new secret codes, is he still playing the game?

Well, yes. But he's playing the game from outside the game. He's playing the *meta*game. He has an entirely new perspective on the gaming experience. Like the child with a remote control who is now actively watching "the television" instead of passively absorbing TV programming, the young gamer has undergone a kind of renaissance. He is enjoying the original characters and action of the game from outside the original rule set. Is there a loss of innocence? Yes. But there's also an increase in perspective. In fact, many kids download the cheat codes for games only *after* they have played the entire game once through with no special help. Gaining the secret codes renews the original gaming experience for them in a new context: that of the game programmer. The next step is to create new versions and levels of the game for oneself. Thousands of kids do this every day—for the games to which they have access to the code.

Renaissances involve similar leaps in perspective, where those who formerly accepted the rules of a given situation feel suddenly capable of rewriting those rules for themselves. They realize how laws they accepted as "givens" were actually choices made by people who had access to the original codes. Renaissances are inherently iconoclastic because they allow people to deconstruct ideas, institutions, and systems of belief that were previously sacrosanct.

This is why the invention of a renaissance technology such as movable type resulted in the Protestant Reformation. With new, personal access to the text of the Bible, passively accepting Catholics were now free to interpret their religion for themselves. The religious wars that followed were a rene-gotiation, albeit a violent one, of the theistic rules by which they wanted to live.

Likewise, the proliferation of a global media space and the Internet led to a battle over just what "new media" would mean. For some, it meant a political revolution, in which the integrity of obsolete nation-states would be eroded through the newfound communicative ability of people from around the world. Indeed, most historians would agree that the fall of the Berlin Wall and the demise of South African apartheid were hastened by the spread of Western media. But it was the job of Net activists, through their published essays, on-line discussions, television appearances, and university lectures, to promote this perception of the Internet as the great social equalizer. Others saw in the Internet an unprecedented opportunity for direct marketing, business investment, or military superiority and used the op-ed pages, business channels, and bully pulpit to promote their own views of a new world order.

Renaissances, then, are windows of opportunity—momentary shifts in perspective when the narratives we use to understand our reality are up for discussion. We know full well that our experience of mastery—of being in on the metagame—is only temporary. It is like a mystical experience or state of knowing. Before long, the pieces will fall back into place and a new narrative will be accepted, most likely as yet another sacred and inviolable truth. This is why there's such a scramble for authority. Whichever old ideas we want to be carried into the next age, we plant during these renaissance moments, from neoclassical and Gothic Revival to the new rules of the new economy and the New Age movement.

So much for the "rebirth of old ideas" side of renaissance, but what about the "new context"? Are we making any progress as we step outside the rules of games? Do the new rules and narratives that we write any more efficiently, or humanely, organize our activities and experiences? Will a renaissance in the practice of Judaism necessarily lead to a renaissance in our ethics and theology?

I think so. Renaissances are leaps forward in our ability to experience dimension. The shifts we have already experienced moved our civilization from a literal stage, through a metaphoric stage, to what I've called a "recapitulation stage," along with our ability to conceive the world with greater dimensionality.

Many of our inventions and symbol systems pass through these stages as well, affording us greater control and flexibility over their use. Written language, for example, began as pictures, or cave paintings. These were literal representations of things. As text developed, simpler, standardized symbols, or glyphs, were used to represent the same objects. A picture of an ox followed by a picture of water might have meant that the ox is to be found near the water. Glyphs were symbolic, metaphoric representations of things they referred to. The development of the alphabet took these same pictures but used them in a new way. The picture of a ox, *aleph* in Hebrew, became the symbol for the sound "ah" at the beginning of the word. The glyph for water, *mayim* in Hebrew, became the sound for "M"—a squiggle in our own alphabet still reminiscent of the waves it once represented. Today, we have little conscious awareness of the metaphoric origins of our letters, but we can string them together into myriad coded combinations that recapitulate the functions of their drawn predecessors.

Judaism, too, started in a literal phase, then reinvented itself through metaphor: in the rabbinic era, the metaphor of prayer replaced the literal act of sacrifice. Likewise, the parables of Jesus also served as allegories or metaphors—ways that many different people could relate to the same point. (That's the mathematical definition of a parabola.) So what would constitute Judaism's next leap? Phrased another way, what is the fractal or Internet version of Judaism? What is its "recapitulation" phase, and how do we get there?

The way we always have: by opening the very source of our religion to scrutiny and reinvention.

Perhaps the best contemporary example of such an ethic in practice is to be found in the "open source" computer programming community. Faced with the restrictive practices of the highly competitive software developers, and the pitifully complex and inefficient operating systems such as Microsoft Windows that this process produces, a global network of programmers decided to adopt a better development philosophy—one based in the original values of the shareware software community. They concluded that proprietary software is crippled by the many efforts to keep its underlying code a secret and locked down. As a result, many users don't even know that a series of arbitrary decisions have been made about the software they use. They don't know it can be changed; they simply adjust.

By publishing software along with its code, open source developers invite other programmers to correct their mistakes and improve upon the work as a whole. Rather than competing, they collaborate. They don't hide the way their programs work. As a result, everyone is invited to change the underlying code, and the software can evolve with the benefit of multiple points of view.

A Jewish renaissance, too, will demand that we dig deep into the very code of our religion, then reexperience it in the context of full modernity. It will require us to assume, at least temporarily, that nothing at all is too sacred to be questioned, reinterpreted, and modified. But in doing so, we will make ourselves ready to bring Judaism through its current crisis and into its next phase of expression. And, perhaps ironically, we'll be engaging ourselves in Judaism's most time-honored tradition.

OPEN SOURCE JUDAISM?

An open source religion would work the same way as open source software development: it is not kept secret or mysterious at all. Everyone contributes to the codes we use to comprehend our place in the universe. We allow our religion to evolve based on the active participation of its people. We internalize and engineer Jewish laws and ideas as adults, rather than following them by rote, as children. We come to realize that the writings and ideas of Judaism are not set in stone, but invitations to inquire, challenge, and evolve. Together, as a community, we define Judaism as the ongoing resolution of our individual sensibilities.

This is the great lesson of holography, our current renaissance's allegory to perspective painting. A holographic plate—like the little shiny picture on your credit card—shows an image in four dimensions. As you move in relationship to it, it moves in relation to time. By strolling past a holographic image, you can see a 3-D photo of a woman wink at you or a bird flap its wings. But more remarkable than this, if you were to smash a holographic plate into a hundred pieces, you wouldn't see the wing of the bird in one fragment and the beak in another. No, the image of the entire bird is represented, albeit faintly, in each and every piece. By putting all the pieces together, we can resolve the picture into greater clarity. Each unit has one perspective on the whole, but only together can the whole be fully resolved.

An open source relationship to religion would likewise take advantage of the individual points of view of its many active participants to develop its more resolved picture of the world and our place within it. Instead of seeing blasphemy in the deconstruction of the Torah as a piece of literature, we come to understand that the document's true power is unleashed only when submitted to the simultaneous scrutiny of each member of our entire community. Encouraging people to develop and share their personal perspectives on the Torah in the context of its historically validated evolution does not challenge the testament's authority at all, but confirms it as a living document with an almost infinite supply of unharvested wisdom.

Opening Judaism in this way would not lead to the desecration of the Torah or the abandonment of *halakhah*. It would instead allow the narrative and laws to reach new levels of resolution and applicability that could be realized only by treating our texts as fully dimensional structures. We free ourselves to acknowledge the history of our sacred books and their development and layering over centuries, rather than condensing them into a one-pointed revelation that needs to have occurred as a single magical moment in time and space. We unfurl the scrolls in order to experience the dynamic among their many sources, intentions, and authors. Free to relate one part to another, we come to experience Torah and Talmud as dynamic documents, existing in a state of tension with themselves and through which meaning is not simply received but actively inferred.

Take, for example, the language used by Abraham to banish his maidservant Hagar and the son she bore him, Ishmael. She is called Hagar the Egyptian, as if to give us a clue of where in the Torah we are to find another way of understanding the events that are unfolding. Sure enough, the language of this passage is echoed in Pharaoh's treatment of the Israelites. Only by deconstructing and relating the text in new ways can the student of Torah regard the Torah's implication that Abraham's treatment of the stranger in his midst led to identical treatment of his offspring by their own oppressor later on.

In a similarly self-reflective fashion, the Torah's laws inform and are informed by the stories of Genesis. A passage of the legal text cannot be fully understood without consulting the story to which it refers. In Deuteronomy, for instance, the only law dictating inheritance rights concerns the rather rare possibility that a man might have children by two different wives—one whom he hates and the other whom he loves. The law holds that even if the elder son was birthed by the wife he does not favor, he must still give him twice the inheritance portion of the younger son, "for he is the first fruits of his strength" (Deuteronomy 21:17).

That last little phrase gives us the clue of how to find the sense in this law. It's like a linguistic footnote to another passage in the text. "Thou art my firstborn, my might, and the first-fruits of my strength," Jacob, on his deathbed, tells his firstborn son, Reuben, back in Genesis (49:3). For Jacob had two wives; Leah he hated, and Rachel he loved. He chose to disinherit Leah's son, Reuben, justifying his decision on the grounds that Reuben had sex with one of Jacob's own concubines. But Jacob doesn't give his blessing and inheritance to his second son, either, or to the third or the fourth. He reserves his blessing and a double portion of his wealth for Joseph, the first son of his beloved wife, Rachel.

By echoing the language of this story, the law hints at its ability to clear up any confusion about Jacob's motivation. His disinheritance of Reuben had nothing to do with the son's actions at all. Jacob was punishing their mothers. Perhaps Jacob wasn't even aware of this himself. Thanks to Deuteronomy, we can infer the truth. The law comments on the story, and the story provides us with a justification for the law. The authors of Deuteronomy understood that their legal prescriptions for behavior reach dimensionality only in the context of the earlier Genesis stories. The real meaning of the story and of the law is suspended in the relationship between the two passages—their interpretive synthesis resulting in a more dimensional communication than either linear description could muster on its own. It takes the active participation of the critical reader to make the text come alive. The Torah is commenting upon itself, beginning the process of midrash (Torah commentary) and encouraging its readers to do the same.

Finally, this highly dimensional approach to Torah changes our relationship to the stories it tells. By increasing our perspective on the Torah's narrative, we pull ourselves out of its seemingly linear chain of events. We no longer understand it as a record of our fixed history or a foretelling of our God-ordained future; instead, we see it as something that is happening in every moment. It is not a record of Jewish history as much as it is a description of the eternal human condition, from which we may then infer or enact our own futures. Because unlike a messianic fantasy of some distant salvation, renaissances don't occur in history or as destiny. They are experienced in the present. By relating to the Torah not as a linear chronicle but as a highly dimensional object, we unleash its real power as a guiding light.

These are the styles of Torah analysis that were available to the layperson only after the advent of literary criticism in the twentieth century. They are the very same techniques that the European orthodoxy blamed for compromising the Torah's authority in the relativistic haze of modernist philosophy. In fairness to such stalwarts, though, we must empathize with the threat they were feeling to their authority as the exclusive translators of the Torah's wisdom to the masses and decadent seculars. Yet even if their intentions were noble, they were nonetheless incapable of lifting themselves from the two-dimensional map they were using to understand Judaism and embrace a renaissance sensibility. They weren't ready, even if the Torah was.

Consider the experience of a cartographer attempting to hold a conversation with a surfer. Both can claim intimate knowledge of the ocean, but from vastly different perspectives. While the mapmaker understands the sea as a series of longitude and latitude lines, the surfer sees only a motion of waves that aren't even depicted on the cartographer's map. If the cartographer were to call out from the beach to the surfer and ask him whether he is above or below the forty-third parallel, the surfer would be unable to respond. The mapmaker would have no choice but to conclude that the surfer was hopelessly lost. If any of us were asked to choose which one we would rather rely on to get us back to shore, most of us would pick the surfer. He experiences the water as a system of moving waves and stands a much better chance of navigating a safe course through them. Each surfer at each location and each moment of the day experiences an entirely different ocean. The cartographer experiences the same map no matter what. He has a more permanent model, and his is certainly a useful, if limited, tool; but his liability is his propensity to mistake his map for the actual territory.

The difference between the cartographer's experience of the ocean and that of the surfer is akin to pre- and post-renaissance relationships to Torah. The first relies on the most linear and static interpretations of the text in order to create an authoritative template through which to glean its meaning and pinpoint one's relationship to the story it tells. The latter relies on the living, moment-to-moment perceptions of its many active interpreters to develop a way of relating to its changing patterns. Ultimately, in a cognitive process not unlike that employed by a chaos mathematician, the surfer learns to recognize the order underlying what at first appears to be random turbulence. Likewise, the open source Torah reader understands each passage as a possible reflection on any other in the system.

The most primitive attempts to analyze Torah in this way were performed by the medieval mystics, who sought to find numerical correspondences to the characters in the text. But such crude and overly concretized systems of analysis yielded results more like conspiracy theory than dimensional life. Modern efforts in this vein, such as *The Bible Code,* substitute Nostradamus-like, one-to-one correspondences for genuine textual analysis as a way of proving that the Torah predicted, say, the assassination of Yitzhak Rabin. These misguided forms of study are born out of the impulse to work with the Torah as a multidimensional object, but they use the tools of a hopelessly linear age and are steeped in the false and obsolete goal of affirming the text's authority as revelation. Six hundred thousand characters in the Torah confirms, somehow, the existence of six hundred thousand witnesses on Mount Sinai. Tit for tat.

If we are to truly dimensionalize the Bible's code, however, we must engage the active, intelligent participation of our community, without harboring any expectations for a predetermined outcome. We can then evolve our relationship to the text from simple linearity into a holograph whose clarity and resolution grows with each new perspective that is invited to participate. This is not the story of how we dismantle the Torah, but of how it might be reborn, yet again, in a new context.

Such, too, is the nature of a truly open and collaborative religion, which depends on the perspectives of all of its members for its ever-resolving picture of the universe. We don't experience divine wisdom as "out there," to be decided and then disseminated by a few holy priests. It is to be explored and recognized by each of us and then shared and experienced as a collective.

In short, God no longer needs to be experienced as receded at all, but rather defined and embodied through a community. We acknowledge that each individual can offer an essential perspective on the whole of Judaism. We learn to re-create the sacred through our mutual participation in each moment of inquiry. In essence, we *enact* our God, together. And we are empowered to do so by embracing Judaism's most fundamental tenets: iconoclasm, social justice, and the refusal to submit to any concrete, idolatrous definitions of the sacred. Our unifying principle is radical pluralism—radical enough to include conceptions of God that might not even qualify as what we think of as "Jewish."

Of course, this means giving up a lot—especially for Jews, who have considered ourselves to be God's special sons and daughters for so long. It's just like growing up. It's a terrifying moment when we realize our parents aren't gods, and it's an even more terrifying moment for a people when we realize our God is not a parent. But this is precisely the corollary of Joan Rivers's "Can we talk?" challenge: "Grow up!" she implores us. Only an adult, who has fully internalized his or her parents' guardianship, can consider participating in the conversation. Autonomy is dependent on adulthood.

In our successive Jewish renaissances, then, we moved from sacrifice to prayer to co-creation. It is the evolution from a fear of God, to the worship of God, and, finally, to the expression of God. From the perspective of recapitulation, God is in everything or nothing at all. It's a radically recontextualized monotheism. Evolution moves us from the concrete (idols), to words and ideas (metaphors), and, eventually, to the direct experience of pure love and acceptance: the recapitulation of God himself.

But to move into this direct experience of sanctity—a personal and vital expression of spirituality—we have to let ourselves grow up. We lose the illusory safety of regression and transference, but we gain the responsibilities and privileges of adults. We lose the magical protection of our talismans and rituals, but we regain their value as affirmations and focal points. We lose the ability to relegate all the hard study to men with long beards, but we gain access to some of the most intriguing myths and thoughtful laws ever written. We lose the authority of our testament as the sole piece of divine evidence, but we gain the experiences of peoples with whom we have always been in competition. We lose the special status of being a chosen race, but gain the ability to choose a path voluntarily and to share what we've found with the entire world. We lose the Zionist claim over a patch of sacred soil, but get to claim the entire planet as a kind of Jerusalem. We lose Yahweh—the one and only actor who is allowed to play God— but are empowered to enact the unity of the *Sh'ma* ourselves.

LETTING GO, YET LOSING NOTHING

To almost anyone but a so-called lapsed Jew, this description of a new approach to Judaism does not represent Judaism at all, but Judaism's demise. They're probably right. Unless, perchance, the lapsed Jews are not really lapsed at all, but our faith's truest practitioners.

Is it a rhetorical trick or an accurate assessment to suggest that it is the most dogmatically observant Jews of New York's closed and separatist enclaves or Israel's West Bank settlements who have actually strayed from the path of Judaism? If our tradition is one of participation in the greater culture, a willingness to wrestle with sacred beliefs, and a refusal to submit blindly to icons that just don't make sense to us, then the Jews labeled as "lapsed" might be practicing the most legitimate form of Judaism possible today.

Without a conscious stake in the preservation of a particular line of dogma or territorial precondition for the messianic age, those who don't identify with institutional Judaism are quite free to reevaluate their religion for themselves, as well as to pick and choose which aspects of Judaism, if any, they wish to employ as part of an overall life strategy. Their path is far from easy. There are almost no mechanisms in place for nonallied Jews to engage with Judaism in a meaningful fashion and a dearth of communities with which they can exchange their passions and misgivings without a need for self-censorship. An evaluation of Judaism would also require real work and real study. An open source Judaism is not "Judaism light" at all, but a commitment to know the religion as deeply and profoundly as its original programmers, in order to enact its next great renaissance.

Unfortunately, most institutionally allied Jews are much too concerned with their religion's very survival to entertain such notions. Our leading foundations and philanthropies don't see radical reappraisal as the key to a Jewish revival.

Instead, these organizations study statistics on intermarriage and declining temple membership and conclude that their religion is dying. By the metrics they are using, the situation appears dire. But they are measuring only the health of the institutions originally designed to protect Judaism and not Judaism itself.

It's as if a group of people were standing around a withering flower, mourning its death and incapable of noticing that its seeds were spreading everywhere. Perhaps the flower that is organized Judaism has done its job. Maybe what appears to Jewish separatists as assimilation and dissolution is actually the transmission of Jewish values to the culture at large. If our ideas are so good, shouldn't they be useful to everyone? Are our institutions still protecting our best ideas, or are they stifling them? If we were to stop insisting that they be called "Jewish" ideas, mightn't they be more readily taken up by a global population for whom—let's face it—the word *Jewish* has particularly negative associations? What is more important, that the world call itself Jewish or that people everywhere benefit from Judaism? Do we really need the credit?

Our exclusive claim on God's grace is not even biblically supported. This is not at all the relationship that the God of Genesis and Exodus promised to his "chosen people." God is offering something to Abraham's descendants that they are to share with "the peoples of the world." He tells our patriarch that the Hebrews will become *ohr lagoyim*—a light unto all nations. God insists that all people are his children, something Jews tend to forget just around the time another renaissance hits. The covenant requires transmission.

Indulge, for just a moment, the possibility that Judaism might best serve its universal function by retiring itself as it's currently known. What if Judaism were the first religion on the block to let go—at least of that specific map we're currently mistaking for our religion? We pride ourselves on being the most radical house of worship on the street, the oldest religion in the West and thus the most developed. Mightn't it be the most daring step yet for us to declare the absolute victory of our nameless, shapeless, universal conception of God? Can we yet see him in everything and everyone? Maybe assimilation of this sort isn't a failure, but our best strategy for the global dissemination of our values.

A key premise of the open source software development model is that programmers relinquish ownership of their code. Everyone can take it, change it, and repackage it for their own use. Are we ready to share what we've developed—the myths, laws, and culture of our people—with the rest of the world to do with as they please? Better yet, are we ready to accept the real implications of having developed a faith that has nowhere left to take us but toward the universal acceptance and appreciation of our siblings?

There's a beautiful moment in the Passover seder that is emblematic of just such an unimaginably pluralist future.

Early in the proceedings, the leader breaks a piece of matzoh called the *afikomen* into two halves. One, he replaces. The other, he hides for the children to find later in the evening. Whoever finds the *afikomen* and brings it back to the leader is rewarded. Many rabbis have mused that the hidden piece of the *afikomen* represents the many Jews who were lost to us— the ten lost tribes or the forcibly converted Marranos of the Inquisition. We can only proclaim, "Next year in Jerusalem," once those lost people have been found. We might best extend the sense of this ritual to include the many branches of our mythical biblical family who were cast off to become the other peoples of this world.

The Arabs consider themselves the descendants of the Jewish Bible's Ishmael—Abraham's son from his Egyptian servant Hagar. Esau, the unfavored son of Isaac, became the mythic patriarch of the Edomites, a tribe notoriously hostile to the Jews and quite possibly the ancestors of today's Palestinians.

Our Torah tells us that we are the same people. Only by embracing the so-called other do we create the possibility for a new Jerusalem.

Four

BEYOND RACE
AND PLACE

"THAT'S ALL VERY WELL," a middle-aged woman told me after I tested my working proposal for Judaism's next great renaissance at a recent talk, "but the Jews are God's chosen people. I like being chosen, and knowing that God loves us more than anyone else. If we give our religion away to others, we won't be special anymore. How will God know to love us more than the goys?"

This is not a fictional, straw-man argument, but a refrain I've encountered repeatedly in real life, from educated and successful Jews living in modern American cities such as New York and Los Angeles. Honestly, I understand how this woman feels. It's great to believe that you're special. All youngsters inwardly yearn to be their parents' favorite child.

Many children quite healthily entertain such fantasies. But it's not necessarily the best way to relate to one's siblings. Sometimes people who feel picked also get picked on. (Read the story of Joseph for how that one plays out.)

The Jews might have more cause for maintaining an inwardly felt sense of chosenness than most peoples, thanks to the profound injustices they have experienced as the unwelcome guests of others. The Crusades, the Inquisition, the pogroms, and the Holocaust forced many Jews, just like children who are cruelly and senselessly tortured by their classmates, to find solace in the dream of retribution. Injustice can almost make sense if justice is around the corner—if someday soon a messiah (savior) greater than any earthly oppressor will intervene and make things right.

The danger of such messianic fantasies, for Jews in particular, is that they erode the evolutionary values on which Judaism is based. They tend to concretize an abstract God in the form of an all-too-human messiah who will lead the march into an all-too-terrestrial Jerusalem. Instead of encouraging Jews to move forward into renaissance, messianic forms of Judaism allow for a regression into mysticism, passivity, and tribalism. Worse yet, these essentially race-based beliefs have nothing to do with Judaism as an actively practiced or felt faith. They are invariably the products of someone else's perception of what a Jew is.

Dimensional leaps are never easy, but they are particularly

difficult in times of stress. Just as it would have been difficult to convince King Josiah, surrounded by invading forces, to adopt a more abstract form of prophetic Judaism, it will be a challenge to convince Jews today, fresh from the Holocaust and faced with substantial threats from Arab nations, to embrace what I've been calling Judaism's next renaissance.

So before we can begin to consider what Judaism's collaborative future might look like, we must rid ourselves of the obstacles and misperceptions we have developed over years of persecution and self-preservation. Historically, it has been the elite and the successful exiles—those who weren't faced with the daily struggle for survival in a climate of extreme anti-Semitism—who have developed the most progressive perspectives on Judaism. Cushioned from the harsh realities of persecution and extermination, they are less obsessed with maintaining the notion that the Jews' special relationship with God is based in anything more than the ability to conceive of one. That's why Jewish philosophers like Maimonides and Spinoza, who enjoyed a measure of insulation from the oppression experienced by their contemporaries, were free to project highly dimensionalized understandings of God and Judaism that went far beyond the flat conceptual templates of their own eras.

But their insights led to the rift we are still seeing today between what are known as "Torah Jews," who maintain a literal interpretation of religion, and "secular Jews," who are more willing to appreciate Jewish ideals in a variety of practical, abstract, or intellectual contexts. Although Maimonides and Spinoza were met with derision, book burning, and even excommunication, their works prefigured today's renaissance by as much as a millennium.

MAIMONIDES AND AN INFERRED GOD

Moses Maimonides, nicknamed Rambam (Rabbi Moses ben Maimon), was something of a rebel in twelfth-century Jewish thought. Safely whisked away by his parents to Fez, Morocco, during the Almohad conquest of their native Córdoba, he was spared the subsequent persecution of Jews, as well as the murderous rampages of the Crusades in Europe. This gave him the safety to consider how medieval Judaism had already begun to "lose the plot," as well as how Jews might regain autonomy over their religious pursuits.

Not surprisingly, only Maimonides' crudest thinking has made it into modern liturgy. Most synagogue services today end with a song called the "yigdal," which is based on a set of thirteen articles of faith he wrote as a young man. Taking pity on Jews living through the Crusades, who were unable to practice a living religion without risk of persecution or death, he came up with a list of beliefs—such as monotheism and the immutability of the Torah—that he hoped could serve as a temporary substitute for a Judaism of action. Although Maimonides did not even refer to these articles in his later work, Jews who prefer to misconstrue their religion as a set of fixed doctrines still refuse to acknowledge that Maimonides' main contributions lie elsewhere.

Educated as a physician, Maimonides was well studied in the Greek philosophy that most of his rabbinical contemporaries had eschewed, and he saw in it the means toward a more logical and less superstitious relationship to God, law, and text. Maimonides was deeply troubled by the monopolization of Jewish law and lore by a rabbinic establishment that saw fit to mandate donations from the secular community in order to fund their exclusive right to interpret the Torah and Talmud for everyone else (much like the power enjoyed by certain Orthodox sects in Israel today).

His first response was a revolutionary volume called *Mishneh Torah* that sought to demonstrate the validity of the *halakhic* behavioral laws using Aristotelian methods. Fed up with the endless and intentionally obscure talmudic discussions of his elitist peers, Maimonides replaced their hand-me-down decrees with a system through which Jews could demonstrate to themselves the validity of the laws they followed. Using the *Mishneh Torah,* people would no longer depend on their rabbis to translate the impenetrably dense talmudic tracts, but could use Maimonides's tools of logic to make conscious decisions about which laws applied to them and how. The *Mishneh*

Torah is a set of codes that attempts to turn Jewish law from a static template into a working system that can be applied in a multiplicity of situations.

The *Mishneh Torah* was criticized in its day, as it still is in some circles, for creating an oversimplified set of rules that pretend to divine God's true will. Maimonides held that many of the Torah's laws were, practically speaking, obsolete. For example, the rules concerning sacrifice no longer applied to the people of his age, who had no temple in which to perform such rites. He believed these laws were originally intended primarily to wean pagan people from the barbaric practice of child sacrifice to the nature gods and to stem materialism by making them surrender their best cattle and sheep to God. Maimonides's insistence that these laws were no longer relevant and only symbolic in nature irritated rabbis, who saw God's law as immutable. We can only imagine their frustration, particularly since temple sacrifices had already been replaced by the prayer service. The living evidence was against them.

Maimonides went even further with his famous *Guide for the Perplexed,* in which he dared to explain the rationale underlying the creation of all Jewish law. While the *Mishneh Torah* provided Jews with a working knowledge of the law in order to facilitate their own daily decision making, the *Guide* was addressed to fellow rabbis and philosophers. Many scholars still struggle with the seeming contradiction between these two works. *Mishneh Torah* is a simplified set of prescriptions for behavior; the *Guide* is directed exclusively to those who are ready to philosophize and question. If Maimonides was an antielitist who meant for people to interpret the law for themselves, then why would he also create a book that he declared was suitable only for "those who know"?

One way of reconciling this apparent elitism is to think of the *Mishneh Torah* as a manual for the end user, like the manual that comes with a difficult piece of software. It helps a layperson use the program—in this case, Torah law—in real life. The *Guide* is more of a technical manual, written for programmers. Not everyone will choose to study Judaism beyond its application in their everyday affairs. Students of Torah and law, on the other hand, who have dedicated their lives to understanding the theological rationale on which the system of laws was based, will find great use for these ponderings. The *Mishneh Torah* provides a rationale for applying Jewish law. The *Guide* provides a rationale for this rationale.

It is as if Maimonides were aware of Judaism's successive leaps into dimensionality. At the first stage, Jews simply follow the laws. At the next level, they gain enough perspective to reckon with the logic underlying those laws, which allows them to apply *halakhic* principles to any number of situations. Finally, they are to reckon with the guiding principles—the "top-level machine language"—informing this logical system. It was as if Maimonides were applying the logic of calculus to Judaism, relating to it on different dimensional levels simultaneously.

Before the European Renaissance had even occurred, Maimonides was fighting for its most radical implications.

More than anything else, Rambam insisted that God could never be understood. An iconoclast to the core, Maimonides saw his contemporaries succumbing to a literal-mindedness that betrayed the abstract monotheism at Judaism's heart. He showed how Jewish texts and laws were artfully constructed in a fashion determined to eradicate the idolatry that results from maintaining any single conception of God. Whether they take the form of physically realized statues or abstract mental constructions, all such conceptions are only metaphors or models for something beyond human comprehension. So Maimonides proposed his "negative theology," through which Jews were to reconcile themselves with the inscrutability of the divine. One can't describe what God is; one can only list what he is *not*: God is not a man or king; God does not have a mind; God does not have thoughts or emotions; and so on. Since God is transcendent, reducing him to the material or the intellectual realm leads to idolatrous anthropomorphism—seeing him as a creature, with attributes like our own. It might be easier to relate to such a God, but it is fundamentally non-Jewish.

Maimonides saw the theological literal-mindedness of his peers as a form of idolatry, too. It might be permissible to experience God as a father figure, as long as one doesn't collapse this metaphoric appreciation for God's seemingly caring ways into a conclusion that God *is* a father. For God has no attributes that can be named by human beings. God's actions might result in what appear to be an angry expression, but God does not *feel* anger. God simply exhibits properties that correspond to human emotions. In support of his negative theology, Maimonides points out that God even tells Job (chapters 38–40) that he stands no chance of conceptualizing the divine reality because he is only "human."

Maimonides found backing for his negative theology throughout the Torah, as long as its stories were accepted as allegory. To this end, Maimonides attempted to teach his literal-minded fellows about the nature of metaphor. In an early effort at applying literary criticism to the Bible, he explained how when the text says, "God opened her eyes," it only means that this character's experience of revelation was so profound, it felt as though her eyes had been opened by God. Likewise, according to Maimonides, the Torah uses figurative language, metaphor, and allegory both to bring the inexpressibly profound into the mundane realm of human beings and to protect people from the overwhelming impact of directly revealed truth.

Although he believed in the possibility of sudden revelation, Maimonides proposed that revelatory moments were the result of hard work and study. Through the conscious investigation of parable and allegory, scholars might receive a flash of the divine insight that these stories were designed to inspire through inference. Only by appreciating and participating with the text as metaphor can one regard the more incomprehensibly dimensional forms it means to evoke. Surrendering to the literal implications of the text, such as the notion that the bodies of all Jews will one day resurrect to be with God in Israel, prevents the reader from approaching what might really be meant by "resurrection."

This position was a great threat to rabbinic authorities, who staked their control over the Jewish people on the literal promise of physical resurrection in Israel. It was just as threatening to messianic Christians, who, with the help of Maimonides's adversaries in France, collected and burned all of his books. Ironically, ten years later, twenty-four cartloads of the Talmud were burned in the very same square. The Jews' persecutors learned from Jewish mistakes.

But the Jewish authorities didn't see how very contagious and self-defeating their rage would become. The Spanish Jewish community went on to ban the study of Greek philosophy, natural science, and metaphysics, for such disciplines were equated with the contaminating force of secularization. All discussions of Torah and the law on an allegorical level were condemned, lest Jews question the certainty of resurrection and the imminent arrival of the Messiah. Their radically literal interpretation of resurrection is still employed today by extreme Zionists and fundamentalist Christians as a rationale for bringing the entirety of biblical Israel under Jewish control. They believe that if the Holy Land remains in Arab hands, it will be impossible for them to prepare for the Messiah's promised arrival, which according to legend is dependent on the Jews' ownership of the disputed territories.

From a Maimonidean perspective, though, these very ties to literal interpretation and physical geography are preventing many Jews from transcending their idolatrous and one-dimensional version of religion. Renaissance requires that Jews lift themselves from the literal map of Jewish history and see it as a model for something much greater than can readily be conceived. For those with a more dynamic relationship to faith, letting go of the God one "knows" only creates space for a greater one that was formerly beyond comprehension.

Maimonides's works were an effort to encourage evolutionary leaps in Jewish thought and practice. His understanding of metaphor and dimensionality predated the European Renaissance—also founded on the notion of popular engagement in the higher disciplines—by three centuries. Though rejected by the authorities of his time, he succeeded nonetheless in cracking the foundations of Jewish institutional lethargy and preparing the ground for successive renaissances.

FROM ENLIGHTENMENT TO DARKNESS: SPINOZA AND ZEVI

The next few centuries were as challenging to the Jews as any in history. By the late 1300s, monarchs were faced with an increasingly open Europe. One by one, they established "national religions" in order to gain economic control over their people, and they blamed the Jews—the former moneylenders—for a host of financial and social problems. As Karen Armstrong chronicles in *The Battle for God,* between 1421 and 1494, the Jews were officially expelled from Vienna, Cologne, Augsburg, Bavaria, Moravia, Perugia, Vicenza, Parma, Milan, Luca, Spain, Portugal, and Tuscany. And these were only the expulsions made by royal decree.

The Jews had nowhere to go. Many of those who were allowed to, converted. Others were executed or deported. A few tried to practice Judaism in secret, hiding mezuzah scrolls beneath their doorpost crucifixes and Virgin Mary statues. These practices, when discovered, were used as evidence of Jews' underlying racial propensity for destructive behavior.

Some Jews turned to a newly emerging strand of Jewish mysticism called kabbalah, based on a cryptic book, now credited to a group of thirteenth-century Spanish mystics led by Moses de León, called the *Zohar* (meaning "Radiance" or "Enlightenment"). The intentional obscurity of this tradition was developed to hide its true, or at least intended, Jewish nature from outsiders—most particularly the scrutiny of the Spanish authorities. The *Zohar* is itself an allegory, a wink and a nod. It's a way of saying something without saying it, to avoid being found out. A layer over something that was itself an allegory. But these protective measures also separated Jews from the workings of Jewish code and set a dangerous precedent. (Today, many Jews think that the Torah is based on the *Zohar* instead of the other way around!)

Things for the Jews went from bad to worse. By the 1500s, Jews were caught running from one inhospitable place to another, retreating into mandated ghettos and then facing either massacre or another expulsion. They were denied the strength of community, the power of literacy, and direct access to their texts. They were frightened, isolated, and hated. They couldn't help but harbor the most messianic of expectations and extend the kabbalistic myths into a retribution fantasy. Their desperate need for a literal salvation, however, led to their incorporation of some ideas about Judaism that have crippled Jews' theology, culture, and quest for statehood to this day.

When sixteenth-century mystic Isaac Luria first shared the creation story that he believed had been revealed to him by God, many Jews concluded that Luria was himself the promised Messiah. Although he never accepted this mantle, he allowed his followers to preach his new myth so far and wide that it became the most commonly accepted explanation of the Jewish condition in the world.

The Lurianic myth holds that human beings and God alike have lived in a state of despair and longing since the moment of creation. Existence itself is an extended exile—a period of mutual mourning between the unity of creation and the unity of paradise at the end of time. The job of the

Jews—the special job of the Jews—is to bring about redemption by healing the broken earth (*tikkun olam*) and activating the "divine sparks" in all matter. For Luria and his immediate circle, the idea that Jews could bring about redemption may have been understood metaphorically. Exile and redemption are aspects of the human condition, perennially. Meditating on Luria's notion of *zimzum,* God's withdrawal from this dimension, or *ein sof,* the endless infinity of Godhead, can potentially lead to tremendous insights for the spiritual practitioner.

But the Lurianic myth's emphasis on eschatology—"the end of days" when the Messiah will return and redeem all beings—proved too tempting for a global population of cruelly oppressed Jews looking for a way to justify their suffering, as well as a way out of it. Instead of understanding the myth as an allegory for the ongoing human condition, they needed to see it as a story occurring in real time—as a description of their current lot and their exit strategy from it. Exile and redemption were understood not as perpetual themes, but as plot points in a linear narrative. First comes exile, then comes redemption. Before the end of the seventeenth century, a vast majority of the global Jewish population regarded the happy ending of Luria's myth as a reality to be expected any day. The Messiah was on his way, and he would establish a Jewish state in Israel.

While most of the Jewish world sat passively and fearfully awaiting the Messiah, those not subjected to the same level of oppression were free to conceive more creative and practical solutions to the European world's disastrous confusion of the affairs of state with the practice of religion.

Spinoza was among the luckiest of them, escaping Portugal to the more tolerant Holland in the 1600s, where he and other educated Jews like himself, such as Uriel da Costa and Juan de Prado, openly evaluated what was going on in Europe and in Judaism. They ended up developing new philosophies of nation and religion in an effort to prevent such atrocities. These ideas formed the basis of what is now known as the separation of church and state. Ironically, instead of facing intolerance from the Dutch, they received it from the Jewish authorities, who eventually excommunicated all three for violating sanctions against philosophizing about Judaism imposed back in Maimonides's day.

If Maimonides can be said to have prefigured the Renaissance, then Spinoza prefigured the Enlightenment. His keen insights into the relationship of the individual to religion, and religion to the state, served as prescient warnings not only to those who oppressed the Jews by nationalizing religion, but also to those who were determined to bring on the messianic age through the nationalization of Judaism.

Spinoza explored and celebrated the essential freedom of the individual. He believed that one's feelings and thoughts should not be created by an outside authority and then passively accepted, but rather developed from within and then freely expressed. His philosophy was based on the then radical notion that people should be able to think and believe what they want to.

Spinoza realized that neither a religion nor a government should be allowed to control a person's thoughts. That's why they must be kept separate—so that law never become religion, and religion never become the law. The autonomy of the individual—"the citizen's right to worship God as he pleases"—should be the paramount objective of both government and religion, for the mind and spirit of an individual work best when they are free. "Not only can this freedom be granted without endangering the piety and the peace of the commonwealth," he wrote in the preface to his *Theological-Political Treatise,* "but also . . . the peace of the commonwealth and piety depend on this freedom."

Spinoza conducted some of the first extended literary criticism on the Torah, rediscovering the lost (or repressed) knowledge that the book was not a divine original but cobbled together from many sources and fraught with contradictions. He concluded—probably correctly—that Ezra had redacted the five books on the return from Babylonia and that the stories were meant to be understood as allegories, not history. Witnessing the terrible error of his contemporaries in Europe, who were collapsing the subjectivity of religious myth with the very real contemporary suffering of the Jewish people, Spinoza sought to break Jews' dependence on the authority of their books so that they could begin to appreciate the beauty and intelligence of the insights on their pages. He believed that individuals should be free to interpret religion on their own, in a manner that allowed them to discover their natural urge to behave ethically.

Like Maimonides, he realized this process of education might have to occur in a series of stages. According to Spinoza, the Jews were a "common people, prone to superstition." They would first need to reform their religion, basing it on "natural principles" such as justice, liberty, and brotherhood, instead of infantile misconceptions like race. The Jews would have to abandon their idolatry and in doing so learn to accept that each person's conception of God might be different. This would, in turn, lead to an emphasis on social justice. Jews would be free to focus on this world and its real problems, instead of mindlessly worshiping the supernatural.

Spinoza was the first European to promote the idea of a secular democratic state and one of the first Jews to articulate the notion that divine law applies no more to Jews than it does to any other human beings. He understood that the only path toward a universal justice was to abandon the exclusivity implicit in being the "chosen people."

Spinoza's reaction to the injustices of European state-sanctioned religions was not to create a religious state for Jews, but to reject the notion of state-sanctioned religion altogether. This anti-Zionist position, along with his insistence on the rights of individuals to interpret Torah in its historical and allegorical context for themselves, put him at odds with the Jewish establishment, and he was excommunicated. The rabbis were not yet ready to open up Judaism to a multiplicity of perspectives. No, religion was to remain one-pointed—an absolute and singular authority that unified the Jewish people under God. Although the European Enlightenment and subsequent division of church and state were founded in Spinozan ideals, the Jews were by then too addicted to their mythology to entertain his universal ideology. They preferred to enact *tikkun olam* not by extending the Jewish ideals to the world, but by living through the Lurianic myth for real.

While Spinoza was busy writing his philosophical tracts in Holland, the oppressed Jews of Europe and Islam found a living person on whom they could hang their messianic aspirations. Shabbetai Zevi, a troubled young kabbalist from Smyrna, had endured a series of disorienting mystical experiences that sent him on a walkabout through the Ottoman Empire. He eventually encountered a Lurianic initiate, Rabbi Nathan, who concluded that Zevi wasn't a madman, but the Messiah himself. In 1665, an originally reluctant Zevi declared that he was, indeed, the Messiah. Shortly, it was proclaimed, Zevi would lead the Jews back to the Promised Land.

Zevi and Nathan instructed all Jews to perform a series of rituals and prayers—alone in their homes, if necessary—

to hasten the "end of days." Before long, a majority of the world's Jews believed not only in the Lurianic myth, but that Zevi was the Messiah to whom he referred. It was a heady and optimistic time, during which even the despair over Cossack massacres of Jews in Poland and other ghetto atrocities was diminished by the heightened expectation of an immediate redemption. Thousands of Jews sold their belongings and packed their bags for the journey to Israel.

Like the early revolutionary Christians, the followers of Zevi combined politics and religion into a single movement. Reclaiming Israel was both a political imperative and the culmination of a spiritual journey. By taking back the Promised Land, the Shabbateans, as Zevi's followers were called, would not only find a homeland for themselves, but also bring on the end of days and the resurrection of the dead.

When Zevi finally went before the sultan in Istanbul to demand the return of Israel to the Jewish people, he was given a simple choice: Convert to Islam or be executed. Zevi, in perhaps his most ironically Jewish moment, chose life. He died ten years later, leaving what was left of his confused following in disarray.

Unfortunately, the saga of Shabbetai Zevi and the Jewish people's almost unanimous support of his messianic mission has been all but erased from our history books. Were you ever taught about this central episode in our history?

Maybe this is why we haven't been able to learn from our mistake.

ALIYAH OR DESCENT?

THE TROUBLE WITH ZIONISM

✡

Many of today's more extreme religious Zionists use the same logic as Zevi did to justify Jewish settlement throughout biblical Israel: It will bring on the end of days, resurrect the dead, and allow for the coming of the Messiah. Instead of adopting, as most of the modern world did, the insights and philosophies of the Jews' own greatest thinkers, the majority of Jewish people have retreated from the universal implications of their own faith. These Jews think they're protecting the word of God, when in actuality they're letting everyone share in the benefits of Judaism but themselves.

The fault is not the Jews' alone, by any means. Throughout the second millennium, violence and persecution were the closest things Jews ever experienced to the laws of nature. The few times Jews allowed themselves to hope against hope that their position in the world was changing, they were met with new atrocities, worse than the last round.

For example, just when it seemed as though the ideals of the Enlightenment were extending to French Jews in the right to citizenship and even to own property, Napoleon died and the Jews were sent back to the ghettos. What good were the idealistic rants of someone like Spinoza against laws dictating distinctive dress, exclusion from European schools, forced conversion, and imprisonment in diseased firetraps?

By the late nineteenth century, as Europe became a great cosmopolitan melting pot, new forms of "scientific racism," along with innovations in agriculture and surgery, convinced Europeans that they could systematically "weed out" or "excise" the Jews in order to preserve what was left of their national identities. The self-definition of a *volk* needed an "other" in order to perpetuate itself, as surely as weeds are necessary to distinguish what is a flower. The Jews, already isolated in the ghetto, were the most ready example of weeds in the garden.

Jews were a symbol both of the "other" and of modernity—of all the cosmopolitan industry and strange new ways that threatened the familiar comfort of parochialism. Jewish separation in the ghettos proved the point, but so did successful examples of Jewish assimilation into the general population, which demonstrated how easily traditional boundaries could be erased. There was no way to win.

Politicians of Europe's new nation-states were seizing upon the growing anti-Semitism and stoking it even further. In Russia, pogroms were orchestrated by the Ministry of the Interior, and in Germany dozens of parliament members ran and won on anti-Semitism campaigns. In 1895, the Dreyfus affair, in which a French Jew was wrongly accused of treason, confirmed Jews' worst fears as the slogan "Death to Jews" was chanted in open court. (Theodor Herzl credited the Dreyfus affair with his conversion to Zionism.)

The rest is history. Between 1914 and 1945, over seventy million people died violently in Europe, a disproportionate number of them because they were Jews.

Jewish reactions to the climax of anti-Semitism varied widely. Many converted to Christianity. Others, mostly in Russia, became revolutionary socialists. Many European and American Jews joined the Reform movement, which sought to marry a new emphasis on social justice with a modification of ritual, habit, and dress to appear more like "normal" people. The Orthodox arose to counteract these reforms, and then the Conservatives arose to balance those. But the most significant new Jewish response—and the one that led to by far the most controversy—was the invention of Zionism.

Real talk of creating a Jewish nation began in the late 1800s, as Jews came to grips with just how much of a toll modernism was about to have on their people's viability. The most progressive of Jews saw in Zionism a way to put Jewish values into practice: the Jews would create a state that embodied their best ideals. The more practically minded saw in Israel a glorified refugee camp—a safe haven for the Jewish people to hunker down through the coming atrocities.

At the time, Zionism was a largely secular movement, with wealthy Jews buying up as much land as they could from absentee property owners among the Arabs and Turks. It had little to do with religion. The Orthodox were actually against Zionism and objected to human beings taking real-world actions in the name of God. No, they weren't fans of Spinoza, but they did have some memory of the Zevi debacle and, more important, felt that the messianic age should be brought about by God, not Zionists. The Zionists, for their part, saw their hard work as a new kind of *halakhah*. Now there was a way to *do* Judaism without prayer, Torah, or even believing in God. Zionism was experienced as an active response, particularly in the wake of "passively" endured pogroms and exterminations, which filled Jews with an undeserved but very real sense of shame.

Had Zionism remained a secular, practical endeavor, it might never have run into the serious snags it did. But when Theodor Herzl announced to the Second Zionist Conference in 1898 that he wanted to put the new Jewish homeland in Uganda, he was nearly ousted. The congress decided that only a homeland in biblical Israel could provide the Jews with the healing they needed, and they forced Herzl to recite a psalm promising never to forget Jerusalem lest his "hand wither." This should have been cause for alarm.

Slowly but surely, secular Zionism was replaced with "religious Zionism," as conceived by Rabbi Abraham Isaac Kook. A rather enlightened thinker, Kook saw the secular and religious camps as needing each other for balance. A purely secular ideology, he feared, could lead to prejudice or even exterminations if not tempered by the ethics of religion. But, as the early Orthodox had warned, the combination of religious and political goals led to a confusion of values.

In fact, it spawned a broad Zionist counterculture of religious zealots, who believed that the establishment of Israel would bring about the "end of days" and hasten the arrival of the Messiah. Mixing the practical-mindedness of the secular Jews with the messianic visions of the mystics, they came to believe that they were the agents of God and that the establishment of Israel, by any means necessary, was their divine purpose.

Religious Zionists began to use the language of the *ba'al teshuvahs* (returnees) to describe one's immigration to Israel. For a Jew to claim his Israeli citizenship became known as *aliyah,* which means "rising to a higher state"—the same word Jews use for those who are honored with saying the prayers before a Torah reading. The word for "salvation," *chalutz,* was used to describe one who joined a kibbutz, and his work was called *avodah,* the Lurianic notion of being made whole once again.

Even nonreligious politicians grew to depend on this mythic conception of Zionism. It gave them some powerful rhetoric to use in their campaigns, and it sounded authentic to Americans, who—still wrestling with guilt over their tardy and insufficient response to the suffering of Holocaust Jews—

reached deep in their pockets to do God's work the easy way. Israel's fund-raisers did little to correct the impression that Palestine had been turned over to the Jews as a concession for their pain and suffering at the hands of the Nazis.

None of this would have been so very terrible—the ends *can* justify the means—if it hadn't changed the way Jews experienced current events. Using the filter of religious Zionism, Jews began to see their military victories as evidence of their divine right to the Holy Land. The extraordinarily unlikely victory in the war of 1967 convinced Jews that they had witnessed a miracle. *Life* magazine featured lavish pictorials of handsome young Jewish soldiers bathed in heavenly light as they liberated Israeli children from the hands of their oppressors. The firsthand accounts of military successes read to students in American Hebrew schools rivaled *Stars and Stripes* for their exaggerated heroism. Contemporary Jews were living through a new testament.

And what a story it was. Faced with almost certain defeat from all sides, the Jews instead expanded their territory and annexed the Western Wall, formerly under Arab control and off-limits to Jews. These last remains of King Herod's Temple (not King Solomon's, alas) became a holy shrine—an idol by anyone's standards—where the faithful could prostrate themselves, endlessly. Now under Israeli control, Jerusalem was declared the "eternal capital" of the Jewish state.

The thrill of sudden expansion into biblical territory that

hadn't been inhabited by Jews for centuries whetted the appetite for more. If only the Jews could take control of the entirety of biblical Israel, the "end of days" would arrive. Wars weren't so bad, as long as the right side won. God just needed the Jews' help to push this thing along. An upsurge in Jewish harassment of Arabs at the holy shrine of Hebron—the site of an Arab massacre of Jews back in 1929—soon escalated the long-standing local antagonism there. In 1968, a retaliatory Arab grenade led the Israeli government to establish an enclave in the region, and thus the first West Bank "settlement" was born. It seemed to many as if prophecy were really coming true.

Widespread Jewish acceptance of religious Zionism also changed the politics of Israel. Ministers who exploited the language of religious extremism to raise money and voters' expectations soon learned that they had to cater to the men whose language they were borrowing. Without a clear majority in the Knesset, both the right-wing Likud and left-wing Labor Parties were required to accept the agendas of religious extremists into their platforms. After the first victory of Likud, Menachem Begin bowed at the feet of Rabbi Zevi Judah Kook, the elder Kook's son—a fanatic who twisted his father's ideas into a new kind of Jewish fundamentalism.

The most extreme new Kookists wanted to blow up the Arab Dome of the Rock in Jerusalem, believing that such an action would precipitate a war between the United States and the USSR and force divine intervention. Others, like the rabbis of

Maimonides's era, believed they should be free to study in the safety of their shuls while less divinely connected secular Jews served as the soldiers who took back all of Israel in God's name. (Such is the law in Israel today; certain Orthodox sects— often the most rhetorically militarist—are exempt from military service. While the majority of Israelis see such laws as unfair, their continued sense that the Orthodox are holding down the religious fort, combined with the political realities of parliamentary government, keep these theocratic rulings in place.)

Even the prospect of peace became anathema to the Zionist extremists who now saw the redemption of the Jewish race as the sole purpose of Israel. After the Camp David Accords, in which Israel agreed to return Sinai to Egypt, Moshe Levinger, an outspoken and influential settler known as "the new Maccabee," declared that Zionists had been infected by the "virus of peace." In response, Begin announced twenty new West Bank settlements.

In short, Israel became equated in official government rhetoric and pro-Israeli sentiment with the redemption of the Jewish people, and Zionism grew from a way to protect the oppressed into a holy war. Religious extremists gained so much control of Israeli politics that by the 1980s they had the ability to swing policy. (The few political leaders who resist, such as Yitzhak Rabin, are rewarded with "death warrants" by extremist rabbis.) Americans today who want to support Israel in its quest to maintain a safe homeland for Jews must also take into account the fact that its leaders allow fundamentalists to dictate a good portion of foreign and domestic policy.

Not that the Palestinians or any other of Israel's nondemocratic Arab neighbors have a more enlightened position. Ehud Barak's proposed concessions to Yasser Arafat under President Clinton's pressure in late 2000 were rejected unilaterally, even though they met almost all of the Palestinians' stated demands. Arafat refused even to make a counteroffer, lest it be accepted and the larger war against Israel's existence ended. Whenever the Palestinian leadership does inch toward peace, radical factions reverse it (and then some) with new levels of violence.

This repeated cycle of hope, compromise, and then more carnage disillusions Israel's otherwise progressive majority. Believing that they have seen the Palestinians' true colors, Israelis elect hawks, such as Likud leader Ariel Sharon, who institute renewed aggression in the name of security. Each new suicide bombing against Israel galvanizes support for military incursions into the West Bank, which in turn fosters the mentality of hate being taught to Palestinian schoolchildren. Meanwhile, submerged European anti-Semitism is given new reason to surface and any residual guilt over centuries of Jewish persecution assuaged by the plentiful new evidence of the "real" Jewish character. Unilateral decrees against Israel—made by groups ranging from student coalitions to the Green Party—further cement leftist and progressive resolve against Israel's right to defend itself, alienating the many Jews in their own ranks.

The seemingly endless crisis in the Middle East and the extent to which Israel's policies are justified using religious rationale complicate everyone's relationship to Jewishness. When we support Israel, are we also supporting the crazed Brooklyners who follow the edicts of Meir Kahane and move to the Hebron, gun in hand? Does our money go to the enlightened society of Israeli people pushing progressive Jewish ideals or to the Haredim, who, in the manner of the Taliban, throw rocks at cars on the Sabbath and attack the houses of people whose wives dress "immodestly"? Is Israeli policy held hostage to the agendas of Jewish fundamentalists and misguided West Bank settlers? Even if it is, how can we give up on our people's homeland, particularly when it is under merciless attack?

Today, perhaps surprisingly, it is fundamentalist American Christians who sponsor a majority of Jewish immigration to Israel. Their literal interpretation of the Bible's prerequisites for Armageddon demands that Israel be under Jewish control in order for the Messiah to come, so they pay for Russian Jews to emigrate and settle in Israel. From our perspective as Jews, it is easy to criticize this overly mechanistic sensibility. But has this become our position as well? For most of us, and most of the Israeli people, the answer is no. Still, our unresolved confusion over Jews as the chosen race, and our attachment to the notion of Israel as a holy place promised to us by God, paralyzes us in our efforts to reckon honestly with the dilemma in which we've found ourselves.

OUTSIDE IN—

BREAKING RACE

✡

The Jews' occasional regression to messianic fantasy is almost always in reaction to a very real external threat. When a people are repeatedly and systematically isolated, tortured, and exterminated, it's no great mystery why they would begin to harbor notions of salvation. Instead of striding forward with Maimonides, Spinoza, or Martin Buber, many Jews desperately cling to the most literal interpretation of biblical myths in order to preserve the belief that there was a great moment back in time when everything was perfect, and that a similar perfection awaits them at some moment in the future. They dispense with *l'chaim*, to life, and instead content themselves with martyrdom. They create a context for their suffering that makes sense.

But Jewish suffering was, in fact, senseless. Neither the Inquisitors nor Hitler deserve a role in Judaism's religious evolution. These madmen need not be incorporated into Judaism's theological schema. To do so risks undermining the iconoclasm at Judaism's core. Jewish myths, history, and obligation to *halakhah* do not teach that there was some great moment of perfection in the past. There was no better time. The mythic patriarchs turned to Yahweh for ethical standards higher than those practiced by their contemporaries. History has been a long, slow, and irregular progression toward civilization. *Halakhah* is based on the presumption that Jews can make the world a more just place through right action.

The adoption of a messianic legend as a reason for being disqualifies Jews from actively participating in the human story. It accepts, instead, that history and the future have already been written. Jews become mere players in a predetermined story, their roles in Judaism reduced from free-thinking, autonomous individuals to those of genetically preordained members of a race. And the aspiration for universal understanding and tolerance is limited to the artificial construction of a particularized nation-state.

To accomplish this reduction of Jewish principles down to a justification for racial and political purity, the most accessible Jewish themes are twisted and confused into dense, mystical tractates. For example, the cryptic layers of the kabbalistic ladder to God—the messianic recipe for enlightenment—are built on the otherwise lucid myth of Jacob's ladder. The real doorway to Israel, as Jacob learns, is found by engaging with God, confronting one's long-lost brothers, and, ultimately, wrestling with oneself.

In this light, most efforts to find theological support for religious Zionism amount to assimilation of the worst kind. They turn Judaism into a kind of Christianity, but without the peace and joy of salvation—only the long wait. In the name of nationalism, Jews abandon iconoclasm, the long-standing insight into the false idols of land-based peoples. Although

Israel has provided a safe haven for persecuted Jews from around the world, the insistence on preserving its status as a holy nation with a preordained mystical climax has diminishing returns. It exacerbates Jews' already distorted self-definition and concretizes falsely drawn ethnic boundaries. Meanwhile, Zionism has become a mantra for Jews fighting against assimilation. But Judaism itself was formulated as a way of transcending the obsession with physical territory and focusing instead on the supremacy of time and the realm of ideas. What's more assimilated than rallying around a flag and fighting for a plot of land, just like everybody else?

Biblical warnings against the false gods of state abound. The first thing God says to Abraham in Genesis (12:1) is, "Get thee out of thy country." The sad irony underlying the current Jewish obsession with territory is that the religion itself was founded on the disengagement from the land. As twentieth-century reformer and social activist Rabbi Abraham Heschel explains in his many books on the subject, "Judaism must be a religion which sanctifies time more than space." For example, after escaping Egypt, the Torah's Israelites spend forty years in the desert. They are not wandering aimlessly, but following a cloud of smoke as it moves back and forth across the flat earth. Wherever the cloud stops, the Israelites place their holy ark. This becomes the new Holy Land for a moment; then the cloud moves on. The Israelites must endure this process for four decades. Why? To learn, before they get to Canaan, that the

Promised Land has nothing to do with a specific place. In stark contrast with the pagan, land-based religions from which Judaism was created to distinguish itself, for the Israelites sanctity is in the moment.

The story of the Torah ends before the Israelites even capture Canaan. The "promise" itself is postponed, and success is left in question. The Israelites get a view of the Holy Land, but not ownership. The redactors chose to leave Joshua's conquest of Canaan out of the five holiest books. As a result, the most important story in Judaism, the Torah, leaves the Israelites in exile.

When the Israelites do take possession of Canaan and get a taste of the responsibilities of landownership, they start to long for a king of their own. They are no longer satisfied praying to God. They want to be like the people of their neighboring nations, who pay homage to a head of state who can protect them. They insist that their prophet Samuel pick them one. Samuel turns to God and confesses that he has failed his Lord. God reassures Samuel by claiming the failure as his own. He tells Samuel to go find the people a king, if that's what they really want. Samuel looks out at the crowd and picks the tallest man. That's how much the Torah cares about the affairs of state.

The Zionist claim that the loss of nation leads inevitably to assimilation and the dissolution of Jewish identity is contradicted by two millennia of existence in exile. A nation can be conquered; an idea is harder to kill. The empires that exiled the Jews are now gone, yet the Jewish people remain re-markably intact. Others use the decimation of the Northern Kingdom in 722 B.C.E. and the scattering of the ten "lost" tribes as evidence of how people with no nation are assimilated into extinction. But the Northern Kingdom's ten tribes were not assimilated, they were vanquished in one fell swoop and forced to convert. In contrast, the more incremental Diaspora of the Southern Kingdom of Judea led to the spread of Judaic laws and values throughout the Roman Empire, Europe, and, eventually, America. Jewish assimilation may have actually been a form of conquest.

This isn't so very hard to swallow once we relieve ourselves of the other half of the great Jewish misconception: that the Jewish faith is based in race instead of in an idea. Jews are not a nation, and neither are they a tribe. In the face of Jung's demonstrations of the inbred Jewish personality disorder, his former teacher, Sigmund Freud, wrote passionately and per-sonally about the origins of monotheism. His main con-tention—in the face of ever-hardening opinion about the Jewish race—was that the religion was founded on an idea. An Egyptian one, at that.

Using what was then controversial new textual and archae-ological evidence, Freud demonstrated how an early form of abstract monotheism had been instituted, for a short time, by a renegade pharaoh two centuries before what would have been the arrival of biblical Moses. He then makes a strong case for the premise that Moses himself was an Egyptian nobleman. The entire legend of Moses' abandonment by his mother, his placement in a cradle made of river reeds, and his subsequent discovery by a royal family's daughter was a much-used mythic story of origin. But in its regular telling, the child of slaves is later discovered to be of noble parentage! The startling reversal in the Moses story—that the nobleman is proven to be the child of slaves—is evidence that this myth of origin was used by the Jews to claim Moses as one of their own. In fact, according to Freud and a good many historians, Moses was an Egyptian reviving what had become an underground mono-theistic cult. Looking for a people to help him forge a new civilization based on monotheistic principles, he found his most likely candidates in the oppressed workers of Goshen.

Archaeological evidence also suggests that the Israelites were not a distinct race, originally from Canaan and then sub-jected to bondage by the Egyptians, but a disparate group of desert tribes. The Torah relates that Moses went first to Midian and took a wife there before returning to liberate his people from bondage, leading many to suggest that this wasn't even the same Moses who left Egypt in the first place. Once in the desert, Moses is instructed in the creation of law by a Midianite priest, his father-in-law, Jethro. The laws for the organization of justice aren't even in the same dialect as the text surrounding them. (Another growing camp of histori-ans places biblical "Egypt" right in Canaan, which Egypt may well have controlled at the time. Accordingly, the Israelites would have made their exodus from Canaan into the desert, then returned and taken over—along with an assortment of other desert peoples—after the Egyptians left.)

Neither Freud's purpose nor my own is to undermine the authenticity of the biblical narrative in order to destroy Judaism; rather, it is to demonstrate how its creation involved the amalgamation of the best beliefs of the tribes who were gathering in the desert. Each of the tribes was acknowledged in the final draft, from the worshipers of Aton (Adonai) to those who saw God in volcanoes, whose mythology was represented in the description of Mount Sinai.

It is not a popular view among anyone but academics, because it doesn't promote the kind of mass consciousness on which simpler religions depend. Jewish promoters from the medieval Halevi to the younger Rabbi Kook find power in the notion that Jews are born different—racially predisposed to do God's work. But where is the active choice in that? By elevating Judaism from a state of ethnic grace to a consciously assumed relationship to God, Freud hoped to enhance the autonomy implicit in the decision to live by *halakhah*. He believed that the choice to be Jewish was a choice to distinguish oneself from the masses. To become conscious. As Freud argued, Judaism is an idea, not a race.

The Jews were hated because they simultaneously devalued the reassuring icons of the masses and materialistic goals of the elites. Judaism subordinates the sense perceptions to an abstract idea of God. It is founded in a renunciation of certain baser instincts, all in the hope of becoming more humane and less animalistic. The Jews' loss of their kingdom to the Assyrians, the Babylonians, and then the Romans only made them cling more steadfastly to their abstract God and their book of law. Meanwhile, the widespread Christian subjugation of Europe's formerly pagan people led only to more hatred of the Jews, who were always identified as the original source of these Christian conquests. Freud saw Pauline Christianity as a way of marketing Judaism to the masses and believed this new packaging also marked a certain kind of regression. By putting a face on God and adopting Greek and Syrian cultic blood-drinking rites for the Eucharist, Paul's sect violated the essence of abstract monotheism.

Freud was motivated, in part, by his desire to quell the rampant anti-Semitism of the Nazi era. But his contention that Judaism is characterized more by choice than it is by blood has lasting value for us today, as we fight our own false racial identity.

We find no strong evidence of racial continuity in Torah; it is always outsiders who make the accusation of Jewish ethnicity. In the Torah, it is not God but the oppressive Pharaoh who first calls the Israelites "a people" (*am Yisrael*), because he fears they might breed uncontrollably (like swarming insects) and then not support him in times of war. From the Amalekites to Haman, angry outsiders are responsible for casting the federation of Yahweh-worshiping peoples as belonging to a single and contemptible bloodline. The Jews' own prayerful evocations of the mythic ideological forefathers, Abraham, Isaac, and Jacob, do not lose their power when these heroes are elevated from mere grandparents to the founders of the Jewish choice. Contemporary Jews are likewise elevated to become the willful bearers of a universal truth. Those who insist on maintaining the literal notion of a shared genetic patriarchy must also remember that the matriarchs always come from other tribes. Ruth "the Moabite," like many other of the Bible's foreign heroines, offered her own fertility just when it appeared the Israelites' bloodline was going to die out. Moses' own wife, Zipporah, was a dark-skinned Ethiopian and the daughter of a Midianite priest. To the Jews of the Bible, at least, it is more important that ideas are passed on than a specific set of genes.

In Jewish history, just as in Jewish myth, it is anti-Semites who first characterize Jews as a race. The Jews then accept this false label as their own. The word *Jew* is a Greek derivation of a tribal name for the sons of Judah, conceived in prejudice and then assumed by the Israelites on their return from Babylonia—their first truly exilic encounter. Reviled foreigners, the Israelites came to see themselves as others did—as a race. It was only on the return to Judea that Ezra forbade Jews from marrying Samaritans, Israelites from the failed Northern Kingdom. I'd also submit that the Torah's graphic depictions of priests murdering young Jewish men for intermingling with Midianite women—an absurd incongruity given the Torah's well-substantiated and openly credited foundations in Midianite culture and law—may have been added by Ezra at this juncture, in a xenophobic reaction to the prejudice he had witnessed and experienced.

The Romans, Crusaders, Inquisitors, Cossacks, and Nazis, right on through the misguided executors of the McCarthy hearings, were each, in their own way, incapable of contending with the "Jewish question." They found it much easier to see these stiff-necked troublemakers as a race than as thinking human beings with ideas that would spread naturally.

European racial anti-Semitism (as opposed to regular Jew-hating) was born in fifteenth-century Spain. Jews who converted to Christianity instead of leaving Spain ended up integrating into Spanish society and becoming quite successful. Spanish fear of a rising new class of people, ready to compete for a seemingly limited pot of wealth, forced lawmakers to come up with a new justification for persecuting the Jews. They decided that converted Jews were not truly Christian—no matter what religion they practiced—because their blood was Jewish blood. Jews were still members of a despised and damned race, regardless of their outward beliefs and habits.

Later, it was Hitler—using justifications created, in part,

by Carl Jung in his most anti-Semitic period—who separated the Jewish people on racial grounds from the other Germans with whom they had almost completely intermingled.

Arab anti-Semitism, too, is based on these same racial misconceptions. In fact, Arab hatred of Jews is not even based on their own experience of their closest global relatives; it is the result of a very conscious propaganda campaign exported from Europe to the Arab world. Arabs and Jews tended to get along fairly well. Egypt was a refuge for practicing Jews during the European Crusades and later expulsions. Life in Egypt or Iraq was no picnic for Jews, but it was far superior to the torture or execution to be endured in Europe. It was Eastern European Christian anti-Semites who exported the racial hatred of Jews to the Arab world, beginning in the mid–nineteenth century.

For the next hundred or so years, many racist fabrications were translated by European anti-Semites into Arabic. One of them, *The Protocols of the Elders of Zion,* a Parisian book based originally on a Napoleonic satire unrelated to Jews, purports to be a Jewish document detailing a massive Zionist plot for global conquest. It was first used as evidence of treasonous Jewish conspiracy in France during the Dreyfus affair, then exported to stoke anti-Semitism and provoke the massacre of thirty thousand Jews in Russia during the civil war. Then it became the basis for many of the accusations in Hitler's *Mein*

Kampf. Finally, it was translated into Arabic, along with other "documents" detailing the Jewish use of Christian children's blood to make matzoh. This fomented an altogether unprecedented spirit of anti-Semitism among the Arabs, who still use these texts and their invented fantasies in official government newspapers to this day. In the twenty-first century, *Protocols* remains on Saudi Arabian top ten best-seller lists.

In order to gain military support in their desert wars, the Nazis exported their own rationales for anti-Semitism to the Arabs, and the Soviets followed suit after World War II. A century of concentrated anti-Jewish propaganda gave an entire civilization new reason to hate their Semite neighbors: race. The lessons of the twentieth century are unlearned in the Arab world, where an almost Jacobean-era anti-Semitism, based not on experience but on the fears of encroaching globalism, has attention fixed again on the Jewish race. These fears extend far beyond the disputed territories of the Middle East. The Pakistanis who murdered Jewish *Wall Street Journal* reporter Daniel Pearl in 2002, for example, had no experience of Jews. There are virtually no Jews in Pakistan. The famously videotaped execution had no real political or social justification. The killers simply forced their victim to say, "My mother was a Jew. My father was a Jew. I am a Jew." To the men who cut his throat, Pearl's Jewishness was an inherited, racial trait.

FROM A RACE TO A PEOPLE,
AND BEYOND

It may be the Jews' greatest adversaries who have defined them as a race, yet it is Jews who managed to adopt and maintain this view in the face of conclusive scientific evidence that there is no genetic basis for race, least of all a Jewish one. We still have trouble accepting that the motivation behind the heinous attacks on Jews, as well as our ancestors' ability to survive them, is not to be found in some racial commonality, but in the commitment to live by an idea that we've come to call Judaism. Although the concept of "race" is no more tangible than an idea (perhaps it is even *less* concrete a notion), the illusion of being glued together by blood or a specific sequence in our DNA, rather than mere thoughts or actions, somehow *feels* more real.

I was recently at a dinner party where several young people of different backgrounds got into one of those dangerous conversations about religion. One friend of mine brought up the question of Jewish evangelism. "If Judaism is so great," he asked, "then why can't you go out and talk about it? Convert others?"

A young woman, a recent returnee, replied in Mafia-speak: "Because it's a *cosa nostra*." Our thing. But what, exactly, does "our" mean? Our race? What about the millions of descendants of former Jews who were forcibly converted to Islam or Christianity? Are they still "ours," too? And what is this "thing," exactly? Some kind of birthright? Something given to us, and only us, by God? If so, why do we bother to study it? No, in Judaism there is no real *cosa,* and there is certainly not any *nostra.* There never was.

By relinquishing our claim to an "original religion," passed to us directly from the biblical character God, we can once again make Judaism available to all who might benefit from its profound focus on ideals over ethnicity. Acknowledging the many influences from which our insights spring does not weaken them, or us, in the least. It invites other peoples to consider their own relationship to Judaism in an entirely new context and, more important, frees us of the crippling tendency to lie to ourselves about the mythic origins of the much more real and ongoing choice to be Jewish.

In fact, the Jews are an amalgamation of many peoples, all united by an evolving culture and a set of ideas. And not even these ideas are uniquely Jewish, but borrowed and adapted from the many cultures in which we have lived. The account of creation in Genesis was derived from a much older Mesopotamian myth, while much of the legend of Noah came from the earlier story of Gilgamesh. The order of the Passover seder is based on the structure of a traditional Greek festival meal—from the egg to the *afikomen.* We find the "Jewishness" in these stories and holidays not by insisting on their originality, but through discovering how they were adapted to serve a uniquely Jewish purpose.

Purim, adapted from a celebration of the renewal of fertility thanks to a rapprochement between the gods Marduk and Ishtar, is transformed through Jewish ideology into the story of Mordechai and Esther. The former fertility rite becomes the celebration of mythic win for social justice, as an evil and anti-Semitic prime minister is brought down by two decidedly assimilated Jews. Though living among Persians as Persians, the two cousins find they are still Jewish enough to be incapable of bowing down to a tyrant who would play God.

Does it undercut Judaism to admit that the Sabbath transforms a mandatory pagan quarter-moon festival into a labor holiday? Not at all. More than a lesson learned in slavery, the Sabbath marks the early Jewish effort to transform from a people who sanctified the land, in the performance of agricultural rites, to a people who sanctified the passage of time. As Rabbi Heschel explains in his classic book, *The Sabbath*, "We must not forget that it is not a thing that lends significance to the moment; it is the moment that lends significance to the thing."

How is it threatening to the idea of Judaism that the Feast of Weeks, a harvest festival, evolved into Shavuot, a celebration of receiving the Torah? Is it disparaging to learn that the Feast of the Tabernacles, a vintage holiday, served as the original model for Sukkot—a remembrance of how the Jews dwelled in booths in the wilderness? Or that Rosh Hashanah, once a Canaanite New Year's scapegoat festival designed, ultimately, to confirm the godlike power of the king, has been adapted through Judaism to become a celebration of the sparing of sacrificed sons? It is rather to the credit of Jewish ideas. By recontextualizing these ancient holidays, Jews replaced their dependence on the fickle and demanding gods of the land and weather with a new relationship to history, ethics, and social justice. Only by exploring the genuine, foreign roots of these holidays can we come to discover what about them is truly Jewish.

Jews whose very identity is wrapped up in the false belief that their holidays are somehow originally "Jewish" refute all evidence adaptation as merely coincidental. They are missing the point. They are accepting a booby prize of mythic authority, while denying themselves the invitation to understand Judaism as the process through which the profane, idolatrous, or inhumane is rendered sacred. They take Judaism at face value, as a set of events to believe in, rather than as a living system of ideas to be energized and actualized through the ongoing participation of its ever-expanding circle of advocates.

The abandonment of racehood calls the whole threat of assimilation into question. In many instances throughout Jewish history, assimilation has been regarded not as a danger to be avoided, but as a strategy. It is the way Jews promote pluralism, strive toward universality, and keep the boundaries that define Jewishness more porous. In the Torah, intermarriage is not a crime, but a blessing. As we have seen, many of the matriarchs, on whom the mythic lineage of Jews depends, were not Israelites at all. (So much for matrilineal descent.) The Jews have perpetuated themselves not by shunning, but by embracing "the other," in custom and in marriage. Assimilation is treated throughout the Torah as a blessing. "Love the stranger," the Torah commands not once but over forty times, "for you were once strangers in Egypt."

In the process of embracing the deepest truth of our tradition, we transform Judaism into our gift to other peoples. Yes, I can still hear the words of that woman who insisted on remaining one of God's sole "chosen people." But even this special relationship to God is qualified in the Torah: Jews are only a means toward bringing new people into the Jewish way. In Genesis (22:18), God does indeed promise Abraham that his own offspring will flourish. But he quickly adds that this state of grace will be transmitted so "that all the nations of the world shall be blessed through your descendants." In Exodus (19:4), the Jews are chosen by God—but only to be a "nation of priests," implying that Jews should be ministering their ideals to other peoples. By Isaiah (42:6), the role of Jews as *ohr lagoyim,* a "light unto nations," is made explicit: "And I will establish you as a Covenant of the people, for a light unto the nations." Owning Judaism means owning up to the responsibility to share it with everyone.

CREATION VS. EMERGENCE

✡

Bad times tend to make Jews think of themselves as a singular nation of people. The worse things get, the more bonded to one another Jews grow. Unity in times of trouble helps Jews persevere as a unique civilization. But this same unity can compromise the universal quality of the ideas Jews cherish. Treated like a nation, Jews respond like a nation; attacked as a race, Jews respond as a race—even though the tradition treats both nation and race as mere social constructions. False idols.

In order to extract ourselves from the reality that has been created for us by our detractors, we must distinguish between the continuance of our very abstract religion and the survival of its often persecuted collection of advocates.

Jewish intellectual reactions to the inexplicable atrocities of anti-Semitism tend to confuse attacks on the Jewish people with attacks on Judaism. Emil Fackenheim, a leading post-Holocaust theologian, has argued that without the establishment of Israel after World War II, Judaism would have perished. The Jews would have been too demoralized by the Holocaust, he explains, to carry on the Jewish religion. I'm not certain this is the case.

The threat to the Jewish people and threat to the Jewish

idea are two different things. And so is the extension and preservation of the Jewish idea different from preserving those people who choose to live by its implications. Judaism is a shared philosophy, developed collectively but experienced quite individually. When things are going well, every Jew feels the privilege of enjoying his or her own relationship to God. The abstractness of Jewish tenets and the portable ethics of *halakhah* are what make this diversity of experience possible. Jews enjoy an advanced and often nonlocalized sort of community. Though Jews have lived this way quite naturally for a couple of thousand years, it's a phenomenon that is only now coming to be understood by scientists and sociologists. The theory they use to describe the natural self-organization of a community is called "emergence."

Until rather recently, most of us thought of a colony of beings—say, ants—as receiving their commands from the top—the queen. It turns out that this is not the way individuals in the complex insect society know what to do. It is not a hierarchical system. They don't receive orders the way soldiers do in the army. The amazing organization of an anthill emerges from the bottom up, in a collective demonstration of each ant's evolved instincts. In a sense, it is not organized at all, since there is no central bureaucracy. The collective behavior of the colony is an emergent phenomenon.

Likewise, the slime mold growing in damp fields and forests all around us can exhibit remarkably coordinated behavior. Most of the time, the sludgelike collections of microorganisms go about their business quite independently of one another, each one foraging for food and moving about on its own. But when conditions worsen—food becomes scarce or the forest floor becomes dry—the formerly distinct creatures coalesce into a single being. The large mass of slime moves about, amassing the moisture of the collective, until it finds a more hospitable region of forest, and then it breaks up again into individual creatures. The collective behavior is an emergent trait, learned through millennia of evolution—but it is activated only when the group is under threat. The processes allowing for these alternative strategies are still being scrutinized by scientists, who are only beginning to come to grips with the implications of these findings in understanding other emergent systems from cities to civilizations.

While I won't suggest that the Jewish people be equated with slime, there might be something we can learn about ourselves from their behavior. We, too, are members of a society with emergent properties. Judaism developed out of the amalgamation of a wide variety of beliefs and customs, all organized around a central premise of iconoclasm, abstract monotheism, and social justice. Our iconoclasm and monotheism insure that we never surrender central authority to anyone or anything. Our mandate for social justice guarantees the equal right of each member to thrive. When things are going well, we feel at liberty to experience these truths and exercise our *halakhah* as individuals.

When we are facing an external threat, we band together—as if we were the components of a single race or organism.

After centuries of abuse, however, we might still be in the crouched, protective stance of a community under external threat, even in moments and situations when we are not. We may still be behaving as a coalesced group, instead of expanding back into a diverse set of individuals with myriad perspectives and strategies. Racial identity, statehood, and organized Judaism itself may be vestiges of a collective defense and entirely inappropriate for people—such as the American Jews—who are no longer fighting for their survival in a lethally hostile environment. Is Israel in a fight for its very survival? Would it be if it returned to the 1967 borders? How would it gain the support of American Jews if it were not under such a threat? Even if Israel is engaged in a battle for its very survival against an intractable, permanent enemy, we must at least ask ourselves if the defense of Israel is really the same thing as the defense of Judaism. Is it possible that Israel's seemingly irresolvable battle for survival has become an excuse for the rest of the world's Jewish population to maintain its defensive crouch and avoid bigger questions about what it means to be Jewish?

By clinging to a group mentality whether or not the need for such a strategy is present, we force ourselves to find new motivations for our beliefs and behaviors. Since we are behaving like an organized group, we begin to seek out leaders and to create centralized authorities that confirm our self-image. Instead of relaxing into friendlier surroundings, we retrofit new institutions to justify our obsolete survival skills. We embrace belonging and passivity and find leaders who preach to us unilaterally. Instead of rising up from the masses, we look for ways to descend into one.

Those for whom the air raid sirens are no longer sounding emerge from the bomb shelters only to be called reckless or, worse, labeled traitors. Such is the plight of so-called lapsed Jews, who are ready to express their Jewishness in ways that don't involve the kinds of group psychology and racial misconception that characterized Jews in darker times. Those who forsake the synagogue in search of a more personal spiritual path are considered assimilated. Those who engage with Israel as a living experiment in social justice must content themselves with being seen as "secularized" in the eyes of religious Zionists, who need to place the possibility of such joy in a mythical messianic future.

We may have to give up more than race and state in our effort to bring Judaism up to the present and into the future. We may have to give up the notion of "peoplehood" altogether. The premise that Jews are a unique "people" depends on a faulty understanding of our own history. It presupposes that we have a collective origin—that the one and only God dubbed our ancestors as a chosen race, above or at least apart from all others.

If Judaism is an evolving and emergent religion, then it could never be successfully defined in such a fashion. As we saw earlier, the creation myth of Genesis was a late addition to the Bible—a way for Yahweh to take on the authority of the gods with whom he was competing for devotees. The practice of Judaism, thanks to modernity, need not derive from the authority of the testaments or the proof of historical events; it is, instead, dependent upon the ongoing effectiveness of its ever-evolving ethical template. The "light" Jews are to share with all nations is not a light that was given to them by God, but one that emerged through the collective commitment to the highest human values Jews could muster at any given moment. It is an achievement. Judaism does not teach faith; it teaches active participation.

As Maimonides attempted to demonstrate before he was rudely interrupted, Judaism is not a set of beliefs, but a process. Jews are not people born with a certain kind of blood, but are individuals who make the personal commitment to live in a certain way. This is why true Judaism is the bane of fundamentalists, whose faith is based in the adherence to an absolute and identifiable truth. Jews are not creationists, waiting for the conclusion of a preordained story, but activists, willing to coauthor that story themselves. This determined refusal to submit to authority is Jews' greatest strength. Jews believe in evolution and that it can be enacted consciously.

I remember a conversation I had in college with a fellow

student, a born-again Christian, who was attempting to convince me of the rightness of his new path. He was elated, having heard the "good news"—that there was a God in heaven who had made us and given us an easy path to redemption. He couldn't understand why I was so incapable of accepting this good news and being set free. I told him I belonged to a different religion—one that had heard the "bad news" and was working on ways of coping with it.

I was only being half-facetious.

Perhaps our greatest challenge as Jews is to spread the "bad news" in the least threatening way possible. The bad news is that we may, in fact, be alone. For all practical purposes, God has receded from human affairs. He is as distant from us as if he did not even exist in the first place. At the very least, as Jews, we must behave as if this were the case. We must assume there is no great God protecting us and guaranteeing our collective fate and instead learn to take care of one another.

For what if the worst were true? What if the scientists studying evolution and emergence are correct, and there is no single story of creation that explains our existence? What if organisms really did simply evolve from organic molecules, and great religions like Judaism evolved out of ancient pagan traditions? What if the existentialists are right, and in the grand scale of things, we are no more than the progeny of fungus that happened grow on the face of a rock hurtling aimlessly through cold and utterly meaningless space? Well, then, we would simply charge ourselves with responsibility for creating meaning out of this nothingness. As Jews, we have already accepted this mantle—whether we believe in God or not.

This is the terrific challenge facing humankind at the dawn of the twenty-first century. The recent and quite dramatic rush toward fundamentalist faiths has been in direct reaction to the spiritually unsatisfying conclusions of science and modern philosophy. Creationists hide their heads in the sand, incapable of reckoning with the implications of evolution (that there may be a way out of this mess other than apocalypse and Armageddon), while *ba'al teshuvahs* rush to the most proscriptive forms of Judaism, reveling in the childlike simplicity of God's certain love. Religious leaders who suspect the truth about the human predicament still administer their faiths to others in the manner of doctors administering palliative care to their terminal patients.

The advent of globalization, in all its many positive and negative faces, presents yet another set of challenges to people and races who are determined to go it alone. It's a lot more difficult for a group to adhere to the idea that it has happened upon the exclusive path to God once it has begun interacting with other groups. But how can people who have believed one thing for thousands of years bring themselves into the spirit of plurality required of a networked world? If spiritual people don't solve this dilemma, the market will do it for us.

Jews have a lot more to offer the world at this critical juncture than just another set of ethnocentric platitudes. At its best, Judaism attempts to break dependence on mythical narratives, presenting them instead as metaphors for us to apply collectively, and as individuals, to the challenge of living together. Our experience with an abstract deity and a faith that has none of the comforts of idolatry can be of great assistance to those who are wrestling with what must seem like the erosion of their most concrete icons and sacred truths.

If we can bring ourselves to appreciate, rather than hide from, the fact that our *halakhah* emerged out of our amalgamation and interaction with a multitude of different people, we can share how to find ways of arriving at ethical truths through accepting and adapting the wisdom of others. Even the biblical prophets would have agreed that God has, at the very least, left us alone to learn to play with one another peacefully. Without any parents around to guide us, we have to become parents to one another and ourselves. The Jews have as good a playbook as anyone for learning to do so.

Once we let go of the exclusivity of being God's chosen race, we are finally free to proselytize Judaism. We may just have to give up calling it "Judaism" in order to do so. Might this word itself be an icon to us now? Does it serve us in our efforts to share our insights with others? Could the sacred ideas it has stood for survive without it? Like the Jews of the third century, whose freedom from sacrificial rites made their faith so attractive to open-minded Greeks, might a post-Jewish form of Judaism once again make us the most futurist religion on the block? This would not be the dissolution of Judaism at all, but its finest hour. It would be a way for us to play a part in saving the world from itself, without ever taking the credit. The ultimate *mitzvah*.

If Judaism is not a birthright, but a choice, then all who are willing to engage in the process of conscious and ethical living must be allowed to join in the divine fun. Our commonality, like that of any religious group, has been our shared myth—one that grew out of our practices as much as our practices were informed by it. Our mythic narrative is our metaphoric understanding of our shared experience through time. It is the pattern we have come to recognize—our way of making sense. It is a myth we took great pains to write together, and its ability to renew itself depends on our ongoing effort to participate in its interpretation and development. Now that we must learn to share the privilege of humanity with the rest of the people on this planet, are we willing to share our myth as well? Better yet, are we ready to share the *halakhah* at its core?

True enough, my entire premise is contradicted by the many ways our own myths and customs have always been profoundly steeped in racial and ethnic assumptions. There are as many warnings in the Torah to kill our tribal neighbors as there are encouragements to embrace them. A good number of our most observant members ground their faith and pride in the Torah's plentiful admonitions not to mix with other, lesser, people. Even more of our detractors point to these same passages and beliefs as evidence of our intransigent sense of superiority.

These are the very same kinds of accusations we Jews make against the religions of people with whom we've found ourselves at odds. How many Jews think of the New Testament or the Koran as intrinsically more violence inspiring than the Torah? It's much easier to see signs of racial hatred at the very core of someone else's religion and as a mere obsolete appendage in one's own. In other words, if this postracist view of Judaism seems like a reach to you, imagine how *they* see us.

Five

HINENI

MAINTAINING THE FREE, open, and intelligent conversation that expresses Judaism at any given moment isn't easy. Still, more than any particular tenet or practice, this evolving conversation—and the right of every human being to participate in it—is the defining characteristic of this tradition.

While the Jewish religion bases itself in myths like any other, the function of these stories is not simply to put people at ease. The Torah is more than a heroic adventure through which readers experience a vicarious thrill, catharsis, and then relief. Jews aren't to relate to its mythology as fundamentalist doctrine. The Jewish story is coauthored by all who choose to take up the challenge. Instead of putting people to sleep, these stories and their collaborative telling are meant to wake people up. This requires developing the ability to experience cultural narrative not as mere history, but as an ongoing participatory event. Likewise, *halakhah* and rituals are not just rote performances of archaic and meaningless actions, but the ever-evolving re-creation and reminder of the most cherished values and ideals. Jews put their beliefs into practice and then practice doing that. It's a big leap in the understanding of religion, which is a good part of the reason I'm writing so much about it.

Religion can be a great thing, as long as we don't believe in it. I'm not just being glib. Judaism is a faith performed, not a faith held. Our credo is praxis—the actualization of ideals through their exercise in real life. The challenge is to perform our duties as Jews and maintain the life of our myths without falling into the trap of fundamentalism. We do not rest in the complacence of absolute faith, but energize ourselves and one another in an effort to make the world as sacred as we can stand to imagine it. As iconoclasts, we hold that concrete sacred truths are themselves suspect. As abstract monotheists, we hold on to no single conception of God, but rather maintain an open, empty space in his place. As committed advocates of social justice, we recognize the need for laws and their meanings to evolve in order to reflect our ethical sensibilities in increasingly complex situations. To maintain Judaism is to maintain a kind of nothingness that in turn allows for limitless possibilities of growth and awareness.

Yet those of us who accept this paradox still yearn for solid answers. No sooner do I explain the benefits of an adult and engaged relationship to Judaism than I am asked for prescriptions about how to practice it. Inspired by the notion of an autonomous and participatory relationship to *halakhah,* an elderly gentleman at one of my lectures politely raised his hand. "I want to stop doing the Judaism they tell me to do. So please tell me, what should I do instead?" What could I possibly have offered him that wouldn't amount to a proposal for a new set of sacred rules and absolute truths?

Nevertheless, it might be valuable for me to suggest some approaches to Judaism that foster the actively participatory ethos at its core. Judaism cannot be expressed as a static set of tenets or as a system of rules to be followed. Not only am I incapable of conceiving such a system, but it would contradict the very case I've been trying to make for an always evolving and community-driven practice of religion. I'm not advocating a new Judaism at all, but a new orientation—not a set of rules and rituals, but a process through which to find or invent them for ourselves and then share them with others.

The important thing is for Jews to feel capable of making their own decisions, individually and collectively, about what they believe and how they will practice it into existence. What I can do is share by example some of the processes that others and I have been using to engage in Judaism on our own terms. They're not the right ways of approaching spirituality or doing religious things—there *is* no singular or permanent right way. If anything, that's what they're attempting to convey.

IT'S ALL IN YOUR HEAD

As anyone who grew up as a Reform Jew in the 1970s will attest, Sunday school was much more about the stories of the mythical Jewish ancestors than anything that Jews actually believed. We were told of Abraham and Isaac, Moses and Esther—and only the very nicest things about them.

One year, however, when I was still quite young, the temple hired a smooth-talking, energetic rabbi with some progressive ideas about Jewish education. Each Sunday morning, he would stroll through our classes and ask us to pose him the most perplexing questions that were confronting us as young Jews.

"Anything," I remember him saying. "Anything at all. Don't be scared."

I wasn't. I raised my hand and asked the most perplexing question I could muster to stump the rabbi. "What is God?"

He must have known I was merely trying to mess him up, but when he answered my devilish grin with one of his own, I felt I had found a kindred spirit. A fellow troublemaker. He sat on a student's desk, crossed his legs, and looked up at the ceiling as if to formulate a response.

"God," he finally said, returning his gaze to us, "is in here." He touched a forefinger to his temple. "He's in your head." He tapped one or two of the kids' skulls. "Deep in here."

We sat there, confused. God's in our head?

"God is your conscience," the rabbi explained. "You know that voice that tells you if you're doing something right or wrong? That's God. He's right in that voice."

He looked at me once more and winked. Then he left the room and, reportedly, visited each of the classes and told all the students, "God is not in the sky. God is your conscience." It caused quite a ruckus as children returned home and told their parents about the strange theology that the new rabbi had been espousing.

Three weeks later, the rabbi was replaced. I still don't know how much his blithe response to my not-so-innocent question played a part in his dismissal, but I carry the scars and the inspiration of the whole episode to this day. I learned that our suburban Reform synagogue was not the place to discuss religion openly, and at the same time I realized that if an ordained rabbi would describe God as an inwardly felt sensibility, there might be something to this religion after all.

So for me, anyway, the starting place for coming up with a way to explore my relationship to Judaism was to wrestle with my conception of God. And, indeed, all of Jewish liturgy and literature attempt to reckon, in one way or another, with the relationship between people and God. Our *halakhah* and rituals are the real and symbolic performance of what we interpret to be God's will. Sacrifices were meant to appease Yahweh, and prayer is meant to induce a mindfulness of his role in our lives. Likewise, the Bible is really just a record of a Creator's interactions with his creations and our interactions with him: his interventions, our protestations, and the prophets' revelations. The stories where God is not present still deal mainly with the characters' ability—or incapacity—to enact God's will. They either attempt to behave ethically or succumb to one of the many fears or distractions that prevent humans from contributing to the greater good.

In order to fully dimensionalize our understanding of our relationship to God in a way that is compatible with the practice of an intellectually engaged Judaism, we might begin by rethinking this dynamic in a fully participatory framework. Since we are not starting from scratch but, rather, embracing a renaissance tradition, we can engage with the primary sources of Judaism while using our new conceptual framework. I've begun to do so, and it has yielded surprisingly solid confirmation of Judaism's readiness for reinvention in a new context.

HERE I AM

The clearest examples of God's interaction with human beings in biblical literature are those moments when God speaks directly to his creatures and enlists them in his cause. In each case, God calls out the name of the man he means to address, and the new patriarch or prophet invariably responds with the very same word: *"Hineni"*—"Here I am!" From Abraham to Moses and right through to the prophets, God's call to action leads to the response *"Hineni."*

Taking the phrase at face value, it simply means that the summoned humans have heard God's call. They're telling God that they're present and accounted for. But these people are addressing God, who most certainly knows who and where they are. He's speaking directly to them! So why do they need to announce that they are present? They could merely be disoriented and calling out to the scary, disembodied voice that has spoken their name. But none of the characters' other actions seem to indicate they are so very surprised. They come off as invigorated and ready for action—or at least ready for a spirited debate about why they're the wrong person for the job. Could there be another explanation?

Perhaps our legend is suggesting that *hineni* is the utterance not of the Torah character alone, but of God speaking through that human being. God calls out the name of his next prophet, and the prophet, open and ready to follow God's commands, becomes the embodiment of God's will. The mythic prophet is, in a sense, possessed by the spirit of God—or, in a more contemporary model, expressing the divinity within himself. Alive now through his chosen prophet, it is God who says, "Here I am!" He has summoned a human, who has in turn summoned God into corporeal existence. The Torah may be depicting a God who, coming to life in human form, exclaims, *"Hineni."* Here I am. The unnamable divine energy of our mythology inhabits the human body and speaks through it. "Here I am," he says. "I'm back." It is as if God is delighted to have achieved existence through his human creation.

The other big clue we have to the nature of God's existence comes when Moses asks God's name (Exodus 3:13). God simply replies, "I am what I am," or, more precisely, "I am what I am becoming." He has no real name, for God is more of a verb—a process or evolution. This supports the contention that God's presence is manifest in this realm only through the actions of his creations. He is a work in progress, as dependent on his humans for sustenance as we are on him. He is summoned into existence through a call and response—a dialogue between human beings and himself.

It is no surprise, then, that the Bible has organized itself around these moments of communion between human and divine. The prophetic texts—books like Isaiah and Ezekiel—were written by the visionaries in the heat of their encounters with the divine, immediately after their own exclamations of *"Hineni."* The holy books, whose human origins were proven by historians much to the chagrin of the Orthodox, can be seen once again as having been written by God, through the hands of divinely inspired prophets and scribes. Indeed, every

Shabbat after the Torah is read, it is raised for all to see as the congregation recites, in unison, "This is the Torah that Moses placed before the children of Israel, upon the command of God, through Moses' hand." This little phrase was painstakingly cobbled together from two very distant passages in the Torah—most likely in an effort to prevent the confusion so many people experience today with regard to the Torah's origin. According to what we recite in this liturgical centerpiece, God did not write the Torah. Our mythology holds that Moses did, enacting—or perhaps even generating and embodying—the will of God.

Many Orthodox and Hasidic Jews actually pray in a manner that confirms the idea that *hineni* is the summoning of divine energy by human beings. At the beginning of morning prayers the assembling minyan chants, *"Hineni muchan u'mezuman . . ."*—"Now I am fully prepared to . . ." They repeat this again and again, as a mantra, until they feel that a minyan is truly present and ready for the sacred task of community worship. The group of worshipers is not really a minyan before that moment. It is as if they are summoning God through their own collective incantation. God is not a creature responding to their call. God is an energy that they are embodying through their collective will. The assembled worshipers are to consider themselves a minyan, ready for prayer, only when they have successfully summoned and manifested the holy spirit on which they are meditating. Many Jews recite similar *hineni* prayers before the performance of any important mitzvah. We are, in a sense, creating the space for God to exist.

This doesn't mean God has to be a creature or spirit, lying in wait for the next opportunity to possess a human being. The notion of *hineni* allows for the Jewish God to become as abstract as we are prepared to conceive him. He doesn't need to be a discreet or conscious entity at all. Any of our modern and ethereal metaphors for God or spirit will suffice. Sure, he can be a living being who imbues his human creation with divine energy. Or God might be more of a divine field—a spiritual energy, like the cloud of smoke described in Exodus or the feminine, ghostly Shechinah worshiped by the mystics. But we can also use a completely multidimensional, participatory, or holographic model for God, seeing him as the combined spiritual intention of human beings. God need not even exist apart from us at all. God may come into existence only through the focus and intention of human beings. We might very well *make* God.

Such a possibility makes Judaism's rejection of idolatry and demand for God to remain unnamable all the more important. People with ideas about who or what God is are the last ones who should be entrusted with the responsibility of expressing his will. They'll only bring us to one of the darker implementations of "doing unto others." Our desire to manifest God in this world, checked and governed by a filter of iconoclasm and negative theology, leads instead to our widely sensed obligation to enact social justice—preventing others from suffering what we would *not* want for ourselves. In a way, God *is* one's conscience—the unnamable internalized voice that knows right from wrong. Yes, it is educated by our parents and trained through the practice of *halakhah,* but ultimately it must come forth as a natural expression of who we are. We know when we are resisting its commands in the name of greed, fear, or expediency. But it is nonetheless the voice calling upon us to act unselfishly and for the greater good.

Even if we choose to go so far as to adopt a form of atheism, like the many modern, practical Jews who believe in nothing but the secular humanism of social justice, then the God of *hineni* still has a role in providing us with a metaphoric scheme—a model—for understanding such pursuits in a religious context. In order to live in the world as Jews, we need not believe we were created by Yahweh or that we are following his stated commands. We can just as easily conceive of God as something completely dependent on *us* for its existence. God is present—created, if you will—whenever a person chooses to act according to his higher principles, meaning on behalf of someone other than himself. We grow God, and evolve God to greater and more realized forms, the more we dedicate ourselves to acting according to the principles that we can identify as holy. We create God through *hineni,* by providing him with the arms, legs, and voices to manifest love for our fellow beings.

COLLECTIVE NARRATIVE

On a trip to Wisconsin last year, I saw a bumper sticker that read, "In case of rapture, this car will be empty!" I suppose that little quip meant that my car would still be occupied by its unsaved Jewish passengers. But I was less troubled by the inevitability of my damnation, according to their schema, than by the delight with which those Milwaukee passengers were anticipating the Armageddon. They were looking forward to the apocalypse! Like the extreme religious Zionists of Judaism, they saw the story of God's relationship to human beings as preordained. They could hardly wait for the finale.

This is what happens when people hear the stories their religions offer and then interpret them too literally. Sure enough, the narratives of the Bible's two testaments—like those of many other religions—can be understood as telling a version of the history of the human race, from God's creation of the universe, through the life and death of a messiah, right on to the end of everything and the tallying of the score. If you subscribe to the right story and follow the rules, all you have to do is wait for the ending and you'll be saved. Best of all, the real quandaries of human existence—questions such as where do we come from, how are we to behave, and where do we go when we die—are now a matter of preordained fate. Sacred truths in a closed book.

Paul's amendments to the Bible and Judaism (which became known as Christianity) were meant to give uneducated people—the masses—access to a religious tradition in which the abstractness of God had proved confounding. By elevating Rebbe Jesus to the status of God's only son, Paul created a story to which first-century people could relate. They could understand salvation as a discrete event that took place as a singular episode in the story of their own lives. And they could understand their good deeds as the way that they fit into a larger plan that had already been worked out.

As a way of getting people to behave ethically, it's not an altogether unreasonable compromise. Accepted as a metaphor, the foretold story is even a valuable model through which to understand one's place in the divine scheme. You accept the preordained narrative and do the best you can to stay on the good team. Either that, or reject the story altogether and risk damnation.

Problems arise when one group starts to see its story as the only possible narrative and the characters within it—whether Moses, Jesus, Mohammed, or Buddha—as the exclusive holders of the absolute truth. For eventually, as the world becomes a smaller place, one people's absolute truth will come into contact with another people's absolute truth. When they conflict, so do their true believers. Everyone fights to make the world conform to a particular story.

It is dangerously presumptuous to believe that one's own conception of God is right for everybody. The models we use for God, and stories we have written to explain his relationship to us on this plane, are merely that: models. Divinity, by definition, is beyond human comprehension. To mistake one's model of God for God himself is to mistake the map for the territory. On the other hand, by remaining conscious that our conceptions of God are mere models, we allow for the possibility of pluralism. Whatever model gets a person to behave as if other people's interests are as important as his own is a good one.

Most of the time, it is not people's religious convictions that set them apart anyway. Our conflicts result from real-world power struggles between despots who manipulate the blind faith of their followers. Driven by their own political or territorial agendas, these leaders use concepts like divine right, manifest destiny, or racial superiority to get their subjects to lay down their lives or justify the killing of others. When people relate to their mythic narratives as historical truths with inevitable conclusions, they presume that the story is a closed book. Their only alternative is to make the world conform to their story, by any means necessary.

I've begun to understand the Bible as a chronicle of *hineni*. It is a narrative of human beings attempting to manifest godliness. If it feels as if we are chosen, it is only because of the intensity of this obligation. It is a path that seems to require superhuman resolve—a resolve for which none of us is fully prepared, at least not without some guidance. Children, faced with a similar challenge, rely on their parents for a sense of what is right and wrong. This is why it is easier, at first, to think of spiritually motivated ethics as coming from some external, parental force. It is a terrific metaphor, especially for a people just coming to grips with the profundity of divinely ethical living.

But as we move into adulthood both as individuals and as a people, we are free to experience our mythic narrative as a story that we continue to write through our actions. The record of human history is not predetermined, but amended with every good or bad deed. Myths develop over time, as a people struggle to define their most enduring collective truths. They begin with our most primitive encounters with forces of nature and extend eventually to our relationships with one another. But when a people experience themselves as under threat—whether from external invasion or the inter-mingling with others—they tend to cling to their mythology in order to preserve their very identity. This is when they find themselves retreating into fundamentalism: the locking down of mythic narrative at a particular moment in its evolution. The story no longer serves as a collectively developed narrative, but as a complete picture of the world worth dying or killing for.

Modernity and the rise of the scientific model do challenge the validity of our unifying chronicle, but they also offer us new ways of connecting with it. Scientific theories such as evolution and emergence threaten our conception of a single Creator and the certainty of salvation. Yet they also present us with a more metaphoric way of relating to our working belief systems. The model of natural selection, for example, goes a long way toward explaining why certain species survive and others perish, even though Darwin knew that Mother Nature did not actually "select" one species over another. Freud no doubt understood that there was no such thing as the "id," but he saw how the psyche behaved as if it did contain such a beast. "As if" is the distinguishing disclaimer. The scientific model is just that: a model. The extraordinary rationality of those who use it is based on the premise that they know nothing to be absolutely true. Their model allows them to behave *as if* something were true, until a better model comes along. Its effectiveness is the only thing that matters.

New theories of emergence—some of the latest branches on the scientific model—present us with a working metaphor for our existence that doesn't depend on a Creator or on top-down justification for the great order of the universe. It is proving a more effective model for explaining how we got the way we are. Theologians have long clung to the highly organized and unimaginably intricate interdependencies of nature as evidence of a divine plan. Emergence theory's new narrative for biological and social history holds that this organization rises from the ground up, through the collective actions of everything from bacteria to the populations of cities. In short, there is no single Creator, but a complex of multiple creators working in tandem to develop organizational structures greater than any one of them can conceive.

There is no reason why a people's relationship to their mythic story can't take on the qualities of an emergent system as well. The Jewish narrative, at any rate, is in the form of a dialogue. It is a series of calls and responses—an interactive narrative where human beings take an active role, through *hineni,* in the expression of the divine. Likewise, the narrative life of our biblical literature is offered to us in the form of a dialogue as well. It is an emergent narrative, dependent on the interpretation of its readers for its life and applicability. We participate in its writing and its telling, co-creating our collective mythology from the bottom up.

Embracing a renaissance perspective on Judaism allows us to develop a new model for God as an emergent phenomenon. *Hineni* is the acceptance of our individual roles in this divine collaborative act. It is just one model for God, developed to address the implications of pluralism and the diminishing returns on absolutism.

At first glance, it passes the scientists' test of "effectiveness" by handling formerly insoluble paradoxes. The classic Jewish problem, wrestled over by rabbis and philosophers through the centuries, is how to explain the existence of evil in a world ruled by God. If God is omnipotent, then the atrocities all around us mean that God is either perpetrating evil himself or allowing for the performance of evil in his world. Why would a good God do such a thing? The alternative is that God would stop evil if he could, but he is not omnipotent at all. It is beyond his capabilities. But then is he really God?

The *hineni* model at least tentatively solves this seeming paradox. In a world where God is an emergent phenomenon, the entire premise of good and evil is a meaningless duality. The notion of good and evil forces even refutes the core Jewish tenet of monotheism. Abstract monotheism, as proclaimed in the *Sh'ma,* insists that there is only one thing going on here: God. He has no antithesis, no evil twin. There is only good and the absence of good—the places where good has not yet spread. It is akin to the way a physicist understands the concept of "cold." To the thermodynamics scientist, there is no such thing as cold. It is not a force of its own. Cold is not an energy. It does not exist. There is only heat. What we think of as "cold" is merely the absence of heat. Likewise, what we think of as "evil" may better be understood as the absence of good. It is a place or situation where *hineni* is not yet being enacted. Those who would perpetrate evil can do so only by killing human beings who create good. But just because a candle can be blown out does not mean that darkness is an energy of its own.

Hineni, like the force behind any developing narrative, is pure potential. Readiness. Here I am. It turns divinity from a state of grace into a living process. Similar in essence to the Eastern traditions to which so many have been turning, *hineni* is a path through which Jews may seek to achieve union by transcending the limits of the ego.

Like any spiritual path, when Judaism is understood as a process, it becomes a gateway to investing every moment with awe. True enough, Jews have a *b'racha* (a prayer) over almost everything. We have a prayer for waking up, washing our hands, even evacuating our bowels. We are not praying for fear of what will happen if we don't. We are not warding off the "evil eye," no matter what the new kabbalists may be espousing these days. We pray not to calm our fear, but to express our joy. We pray to bring the act of creation into each moment of our lives. We recognize our roles as the characters in a divine narrative and invest in each of our actions the mindfulness befitting the parts we have chosen to play. We pray on encountering the first bud of spring, sanctifying the ongoing creation to which we are witness. We bid farewell to Shabbat every week with a prayer that resanctifies the divine act of creation, "in memory of the works at the beginning."

The strident optimism and dogged activism so character- istic of Jewish culture—what is mistaken by so many as a form of vulgarity—finds its root in our willingness to participate in the creation of our world. We have assumed a responsibility that many others have deferred to God. Some of us re-create God's creative work through ritual, while others adopt a more participatory model of ongoing creation through the performance of good works. In either case, the Jewish difference is to engage consciously in the writing of our story.

My experience studying media, and my exposure to the abuse of narrative by politicians, cultural programmers, and the advertising industry, has made me suspicious of almost all those who would tell us stories. But I've come to accept the very positive power of narrative when it is offered in the spirit of collective participation. Just as religions are terrific if no one really believes in them, narratives are altogether empowering when we are free to engage in their writing.

The tradition of midrash—the development of new stories, explanations, and parables around the core mythology of our Torah—is the right and responsibility of every thinking Jew. Like open source programmers, we write our own narratives around a central core. Judaism is an act of continual creation. It is based in the remembrance, revision, and recontextualization of myth. The texts become alive not because they are based in historical fact, but because they are being read and responded to. Just as God needs human beings to exist, so, too, does the Torah require our active readership and response.

The only caveat is that this is not to be a solo journey. Although the experience of *hineni* and direct Torah interpretation is intensely personal, Judaism is not a private religion. We are never to engage with Torah alone, but always with a minyan of at least ten literate Jews. This mandate for community interpretation of the text is a safeguard. It allows for the introduction of new ideas, while providing a buffer for their integration into the community's collective mythology. It is a balancing act. We can't avoid change altogether and maintain a living religion—but we can't change so much, so rapidly, that Judaism becomes unrecognizable to a majority of its practitioners. It is a constant challenge to avoid falling into one extreme or the other.

Some of us still want to think of Judaism as an absolutely fixed thing, so that our only job is to conform to its demands and rationalize its inconsistencies. It is God's truth, after all. A perfect thing. The most liberal minded among us, in an equally reckless form of extremism, think Judaism should turn on a dime to satisfy our momentary whims. Whether it's pop kabbalah or the belief that Jews are supposed to smoke marijuana at the closing of Shabbat, the Jews on this end of the spectrum simply bend the religion to support their own lifestyles.

The tradition of community-driven decision making keeps us on course. The almost comically argumentative nature of most synagogue boards attests to the endurance of this practice. We negotiate our collective story. A ritual committee's decision to refuse incorporating the names of the matriarchs into their evening prayers is their prerogative. So was the decision to reject my childhood rabbi's proposal that "God is your conscience." Judaism allows each of its communities to make such decisions for itself. This is why we have no governing body and no official doctrine. Our narrative is the result of an almost Darwinian battle for the survival of the best ideas, tempered by the necessity for community cohesion. It emerges. But the longer we can resist the temptation to settle on a single community answer, the more capacity we have for pluralism and the life-affirming debate it affords us.

Basing our entire mythology on the celebration of life over the idolatrous worship of death, we wouldn't have it any other way. To celebrate life means to accept that there is no conclusion to our story. It is open-ended and forever continuing. Our understanding of God and our ability to exercise divinity is an act of ongoing personal and community improvement. This requires a great tolerance for plurality as well as for a tremendous amount of uncertainty. The moment we sense a satisfactory conclusion is the moment we know we have strayed off the path, for there is always more work to be done. Final consensus corresponds to the death of new spiritual possibility.

This is what separates Jewish theology from the certainty of their more fundamentalist Arab counterparts in the Middle East. In 1998, Sheik Ekrima Sabri, the leading Muslim official in Palestinian-controlled Jerusalem, told *New Yorker* reporter Jeffrey Goldberg that the Jews' great weakness is that they embrace life, while "the Muslim embraces death. . . . Look at the society of the Israelis. It is a selfish society that loves life.

These are not people who are eager to die for their country and their God. The Jews will leave this land rather than die, but the Muslim is happy to die." Insofar as this is true, it is not because Jews cling selfishly to life, but because our narrative offers an infinite possibility of outcomes, limited only by the ability to think and act creatively. Those narratives that are bound by a sealed fate offer their followers no choice but to die in its execution. An open-ended narrative demands that we choose life over death and adapt to the circumstances that confront us. As Jews, we do not live for our story; our story lives for us.

This allows Judaism to be a living religion. It is debated into the future. It is a harder path, in certain ways, because we cannot simply follow the rules, but must take an active role in making them. And we must do so through the challenging and contentious deliberations that characterize any collaborative effort of this magnitude. When we do change our understanding of the story, we do so in a way that remembers the work of those who went before us. Even the rejected arguments of the Talmud remain on the record, as part of the treasured document. Our mythical forefathers carried the broken, sacred fragments of Moses' first tablets—smashed to bits when he saw his Israelites worshiping a golden calf—in an ark with them through the desert. By maintaining our debt of allegiance to what went before, we enable ourselves to bring these old forms into our unwritten future for further reinvention.

RELIGION'S NEW PURPOSE

Before we can map out a strategy for practicing Judaism to-day in a manner more consistent with its core values, we had better look at what functions we hope to have religion serve in this new era. For many of us, Judaism itself may seem super-fluous. As the root cause of so much persecution by others and misunderstanding by us, Judaism may appear more like a vestige better discarded than resuscitated. But Judaism's core values, combined with its open-ended and improvisatory na-ture, make it a valuable alternative in an age characterized by a new rise in fundamentalism. Its unique focus on community practice over individual salvation or transcendence distinguishes it from the Eastern traditions, as well, to which so many of our more intelligent members have flocked. Even if we decide to allow Judaism to dissolve as we know it into a free set of ideas to be enjoyed by the world, we must steward this dissolution in a manner consistent with our tradition.

The difficulty in formulating a single approach to practice is that religion generally serves two main functions, and they are often at odds with each other. On the one hand, religions quell the baser expressions of human nature. They are meant to keep violent, selfish, and destructive people from harming others. Religion is, in this role, a form of social control. On the other hand, religions must also serve to inspire thinking, tolerant people to achieve new levels of understanding and spiritual development. Religion's role, in this case, is to provide the tools for human evolution.

Can Judaism do both?

Probably not. Religion's function as a way of controlling the masses finds its foundation in some very un-Jewish ideas about the world and almost invariably leads to the kinds of static moral templates and fundamentalism that Judaism was designed to avert. It is shortsighted, though not altogether unreasonable, to fear that the masses, uncontrolled and left to their own devices, will rape and pillage one another until there's nothing left of civilization. This view holds that any peaceful society is the result of human beings learning to tame their more beastly natures. Those who can't come to behave ethically through enlightened self-interest must be frightened into behaving according to a set of rules, lest they suffer the penalties inflicted by God—in this life or, more probably, in the hereafter. Like a child who learns not to stay out after curfew for fear of losing his allowance or getting "grounded," the God-fearing believer behaves according to the proscribed rules out of the superstitious belief in some form of damnation.

Although this may have, at one time, proved a successful strategy for keeping people in line, it promotes a blind faith in a set of rules for moral behavior, established not by God but by whoever happens to be in charge. The rules can just as easily be changed to include the persecution or elimination of non-believers or anyone else who may threaten the leaders' grasp on their constituencies. As we've seen throughout history, blind obedience to our leaders' decrees leads more often to violence than to peace. Instead of offering a path toward peaceful coexistence, religion ends up being used to justify the inevitability of perpetual conflict.

Religious control is a double-edged sword. Exercised by benevolent leadership, repression can lead to a certain amount of cooperation, however short-term. But the masses are rendered helpless to make decisions for themselves, robbing the society of its many built-in opportunities for self-regulation. Intelligence is surrendered to obedience, as people become as ready to follow the decrees of madmen as they are those of saints. In fact, leaders who espouse fundamentalist doctrine are rarely true believers themselves. Instead of encouraging compassion, such leaders more often turn their followers into the enemies of someone else's. Believers must harbor resentment in order to justify their own path and the exclusivity of its redemption. Worse, by exchanging their autonomy for a free pass to heaven, many fundamentalists render themselves incapable of divining ethics for themselves.

Maybe this is why Judaism eschews the notion of the masses altogether. There is no word for "the masses" in the

Hebrew Bible. The only humans who populate these stories are called "people," and they are all judged capable of making the right kinds of decisions—so much so that they must take personal responsibility for their actions when they don't. Karl Marx's early formulations of the Communist Manifesto were largely a reaction to the belief that there even exists a class of people who can be considered masses. Applying Jewish logic to the socioeconomic sphere, he saw that activism and social justice were the tools for elevating the masses back to their status as human beings whose free will must be exercised.

Fundamentalism doesn't allow for the ongoing evolution of religious doctrine; it is deemed perfect the way it is. Because Judaism emphasizes life, the religion cannot be frozen in time this way. There is no perfect version of the code. Revision leads to improvement. But how can you have faith in a religion that changes? You can't. You can have faith only in the process. And the only way to relate to a "way" that is in a constant state of evolutionary flux is through intelligence. This is why Jews stress education so forcefully. As the programmers of our own religious codes, we require highly developed faculties for discerning between positive innovations and potential setbacks. We need to remain aware of the many instances, historically, when we have lost our way so that we don't repeat the same mistakes.

Real Judaism is a smart person's religion. Through intelligence we develop compassion. This is not an elitist stance. There is no place for the unwashed, uneducated masses, because their very existence depends on injustice and cruelty. No, everyone must be smart.

Maimonides made a similar argument in the *Guide for the Perplexed,* by creating a hierarchy of human abilities. The "faculty of reason" was at the top of his list. Because Maimonides saw God as an expression of pure rationality, he believed we were created in God's image only insofar as we are able to exhibit rationality. The prophets were, first and foremost, according to Maimonides, men of intellect. Their ability to reason prepared them for their subsequent revelations.

This wasn't to be a path for everyone. Maimonides believed in the existence of the masses, and that philosophy was too dangerous a tool for them to work with. He warned rabbis not to share the "unadorned truth" with those who are not ready. Perhaps this is the logic that today's rabbis are using when they insist on protecting their congregations from the overwhelming historical and archaeological evidence that most of the stories in the Torah never happened. If people are more comfortable believing that their myths are true, who are we to say anything to the contrary? Must Jews deny all literal interpretations of myth and, in the process, refute all claims to messianic salvation? Must we continue to "kill Christ" at every possible juncture?

Maybe the "bad news" about our shared responsibility for the fate of our religion and our very reality is not for public consumption. Maybe the vast majority of people should just be told the rules. But life by the rules is no longer working. It is too simplistic for thinking people, who end up rejecting religion altogether once they discover there is no avenue for their active interpretation. And it is too dangerous for unthinking people, who are now reckoning with the implications of a global society and likely to fall prey to the worst sorts of paranoia. If there has ever been a time to encourage autonomous thinking, it is now. The so-called masses are networked. We keep them ignorant and parochial at our own peril.

These are difficult times to entertain such progressive notions. But Judaism has always taken its greatest strides under duress. The oral law was codified by the Pharisees, in the midst of occupation and rebellion. The Bible itself was canonized during the first century, while Israel was battling the Romans. As we have seen, Maimonides, Spinoza, Freud, and Buber redefined Judaism's boundaries during the darkest moments of Jewish history.

Today, as the world's most uneducated and historically inexperienced peoples once again blame the Jews for all that is wrong with change, we must take yet another leap forward in our ability to conceive the extent to which we can direct our collective destiny.

NATURAL *HALAKHAH*—
A LIVING COVENANT

✡

If Judaism in the coming era is to be less of a means of social control than it is an opportunity for intelligent and active participation in our collective destiny, then we need to devise an orientation to *halakhah* that allows our body of law to respond to our developing sensibilities. *Halakhah* is the codified oral law, compiled into its written form during the first few centuries C.E. Unlike the many rituals that help us re-create our experience of God, *halakhah* is a code of conduct that helps us to define our ethical standards at any given moment. While our rituals concern the ceremonial, *halakhah* informs our behavior in the real world.

In contrast with the decrees of more fundamentalist faiths, *halakhah* need not be based in authoritarian rule or absolute behavioral truths. This is what Maimonides attempted to show in the *Mishneh Torah.* More than a list of rules, *halakhah* is a very logical system that can be applied, with a little intelligence, to almost any situation. We can't motivate our allegiance to *halakhah* today by deferring to the authority of God and the noble past of our people. Even the mythic Israelites who witnessed the miracles at Mount Sinai and experienced the beneficence of God's outstretched arms and the rain of manna in the desert soon forgot these unmistakable proofs of Yahweh's righteousness and descended back into sin. If the direct witnesses of God's greatest powers did not believe in him, we cannot hope to ground our allegiance to the commandments in the authority of their mythic origin.

Our faith in *halakhah* must derive from its ongoing effectiveness in providing sense and order to our lives. It was written by human beings striving to enact the will of God and must be edited and updated by human beings as well. Maimonides showed how the rules pertaining to sacrifice no longer applied to post-Temple Jews and could be discarded. But he did so through careful consideration, dividing the *halakhah* between conditional laws meant for a certain era and everlasting ones that apply in any age. We cannot change Judaism whenever we want to, merely to accommodate our most decadent whims or an ethically lax lifestyle. We evolve Judaism in order to bring it closer to the intentions of the highest ethical codes in its program. The *halakhah* is like the command code of a computer program. Many lines of code apply to situations that may no longer exist, but the essential purpose of the program must remain intact as we develop new applications for new times. We had better study and understand it well before we mess with it.

Just because the *halakhah* may have been written by human beings does not mean we can disregard its power. It was developed, and must continue to be developed, through community deliberation and a great deal of due process. When *halakhah* works, it works because it inspires an autonomously experienced impulse to do good. Sure, it would be easier in some respects not to upset the authoritarian rule of *halakhah* that so many still use to justify their obedience to the commandments. But doing something because we are "told" to is far less difficult or enriching than doing it by choice, in the moment, because we honestly feel it is good and right. The laws are meant to train us, but not as one housebreaks a dog. While mindless adherence to the law is better than following one's baser instincts, it does not encourage the kind of thinking that develops one's ability to improvise ethics in new situations. When engaged in mindfully, *halakhah* becomes the process through which we internalize the logic and emotional fabric of an ethical template into our daily behavior as autonomous adults.

The crisis of modernity, with its emphasis on the individual as the source of all experience, led many Jewish philosophers to consider a more self-driven *halakhah*. The individual was to become the authority, both in relationship to the interpretation of Torah and in the performance of *halakhah*. While this is a quite beautiful and challenging vision for a personal relationship to religion, it may not fully realize the possibilities for collective engineering available to today's community of Jews. The dimensional leap associated with Judaism's third stage of development—from Temple to rabbinic to fully participatory—brings with it an increase in our perspective. Modernism came without such a dimensional leap. It was the last gasp of our second renaissance and a direct result of centuries of rabbinic Judaism, with its focus on personalization over central authority.

Judaism's reaction to the advent of globalism and the insights of chaos math can foster instead a more complex and interconnected style of *halakhic* evolution. It's not that the newfound power of the individual allows one to devise an ethical model, but that the power of a collective allows us to create a series of overlapping models together. By making use of community forums, classrooms, and even on-line networks, we can compare and contrast the strategies we have developed. Our success will depend on our ability to respect the opinions of others and to acknowledge and incorporate their insights without feeling threatened about our own connection to *halakhah*. The legacy of our work will rest in our willingness to compare and contrast our methods in the open spirit of collaboration.

As Brad Hirschfield, a progressive Orthodox rabbi, explained to me, the kinds of questions we ask each other can no longer be simple dualisms like "Do you keep kosher?" Like the inquiry of a bad interviewer, such a question can lead only to a yes or no answer. If the answer is no, then the conversation is over—and one person is left feeling less "Jewish" than the other. If the answer is yes, then it will invariably turn into an argument about who really is keeping kosher. Instead,

Hirschfield suggests, the questions we ask each other should assume the *halakhic* validity of both parties. "Try asking, '*How do you keep kosher?*' or, '*What does kosher mean to you?*'" Hirschfield told me. "You'll be surprised at the kind of conversation that is opened up."

We had just such a conversation ourselves. I explained to the rabbi that I see the prohibition on eating milk with meat as a form of ethical training. The Bible tells us not to cook a kid in its mother's milk. To me, this means not to "add insult to injury." I see the kosher laws as a way of acknowledging the sacrifice that other creatures are making so that we may feed ourselves. Our laws for ethical slaughter, just like the laws forbidding hunting, are meant to prevent unnecessary cruelty to our fellow beings and bring into consciousness the reality of destroying other lives. That's why, for myself, I've extended the prohibition on eating milk with meat to include not eating chicken with eggs.

Hirschfield laughed out loud. He was not derisive; he was delighted. No, he probably didn't adjust his own dietary habits to include my chicken and egg rule, but it gave him an additional perspective on the *halakhah* he did follow. And he demonstrated to me the value in sharing, rather than judging, one as a way of invigorating our relationship to the convenant and one another. Hirschfield and I parted with a sense of joy— we had confirmed our mutually held belief that the thoughtful consideration of *halakhah* was even more important than any particular version of *halakhah*. And we both felt more Jewish for it.

The covenant—our agreement to adhere to some version of *halakhah*—is the most profound commitment made by anyone who chooses to live as a Jew. As best experienced, it is an almost subconscious, mythic pull toward a natural *halakhah*. As Spinoza and later Enlightenment philosophers argued, the potential to do good is within all human beings and will rise naturally to the surface if nourished. As Conservative rabbi and scholar Neil Gillman explains it, such a sensibility does not require a belief in God at all: "If God did not command, then maybe we can discern a commanding voice in our very human nature and in our communal needs, and we may be prepared to hearken as obediently to this voice as our ancestors did to God's." Or, as my childhood rabbi put it, "God is your conscience."

In the one-dimensional Judaism of the Temple era, the direct commands of our *halakhah* prevented murder. In the context of the more dimensionalized perspective of the rabbinic era, the fact that there is *halakhah* at all demonstrates a theological and ethical contention. By living according to an evolving set of principles, human beings can make the world a less cruel place and, through our efforts, improve on nature. Finally, using our current postmodern perspective, we come to realize that our collective human nature, working in concert, can itself command a natural *halakhic* order. It emerges from our very being, as a fruit of collaborative coeducation. Judaism is a path toward being smart *and* good. Better, we are good *because* we are smart.

TALKING LAW

And so the great discussion begins. In the spirit of open inquiry, we leave no stone unturned. Everything is up for debate, and no historical fact about our origins must be repressed for fear of its implications. Let's try looking at just a couple of Jewish laws in this light.

We understand that our laws were developed to help us behave more humanely in a variety of situations. For example, like animal sacrifice, which was created as a substitute for the sacrifice of our firstborn male sons to the god Molloch, circumcision was incorporated into the Jewish faith as a sign of our covenant with the kinder, gentler God, Yahweh. We have been circumcising our male sons as a confirmation of this pact with the Jewish God to this day. Yet, as almost anyone who has been through the ritualized removal of his son's foreskin will attest, circumcision feels like anything but a demonstration of our humanity. Sure, in contrast with the murder of innocent babies performed by our polytheistic counterparts, circumcision must have seemed positively enlightened. As Freud later explained, circumcision also calmed any residual primeval anxiety that new fathers felt over the threat that their sons might pose to the established family order. But are we still subject to the violence such primitive emotions may have engendered in the past? Is the fact that "my father did this to me" still enough to make us perpetuate this custom into the future?

Many Jewish mothers and fathers do not, and they voice their opinions on myriad Web sites dedicated to conversations about circumcision and the development of a number of alternatives. One movement growing in popularity advocates a newly invented ceremony called *bris shalom*, "peaceful cove-nant," that they hope will serve as one of many possible alter-natives "which fulfill the spiritual and communal obligations of Jewish circumcision without its traumatic effects or violation of rights. These ceremonies lovingly welcome a Jewish boy into the community of Jews while maintaining his bodily integrity and his human rights." Could this be true? Would a simple *bris shalom* ceremony really count as having met one's obligations to the covenant? (Theodor Herzl seemed to think so; he chose not to circumcise his sons.) For the purposes of Judaism, though, the conversation itself is more important than the particular decision one makes.

I'm not yet sure how I feel about circumcision myself. But should the day arise when I need to make this choice on behalf of a son, I'm glad that Judaism now offers me more than the stern voice of an intransigent rabbi or the shunning of an entire community. It is decidedly more difficult to face each *halakhic* decision as if it is to be made anew, but this is precisely the challenge of practicing Judaism autonomously, as a faith undergoing perpetual revision.

Take our obligation to engage in the highest Jewish holy day. No, not Rosh Hashanah or Yom Kippur, but the Sabbath. Biblically, the function of Sabbath was to create a time that was *kadosh*, meaning separate, special, and sacred. Using the justification that our God commanded us to make this special day is tremendously useful in a real world, where we must get permission from our employer to take a day off. (It's a lot easier to blame God for the fact that you can't hustle through the weekend for that big Monday pitch than to argue your personal desire for a sacred day each week. I know—it's one of the reasons I started going to temple on Friday nights in the first place.) The commandment to obey the Sabbath lets us turn God into our labor leader. It's a great strategy for former slaves, but it may not be the most forthright one for us to use today.

If Sabbath is meant to separate a single day, we must ask ourselves, what is it that we're separating ourselves from? What, in the modern experience, permeates everything we do and touch? What might we separate ourselves from that would afford us the ability to reflect meaningfully on our situation?

Commerce. Today, we are to be available to our business associates—through our mediating technologies—at any hour, day or night. We live in an age when on-line marketers measure human attention in quantities called "eyeball hours." Any moment spent thinking instead of spending, or laughing instead of working, is an opportunity missed. And the more time we sacrifice to production and consumption, the less any alternative seems available to us.

In such an environment, Sabbath becomes a way of combating the contraction of personal and community time and space. Sabbath sets aside one day each week to refrain from buying or selling anything. Sabbath is a way to reclaim your time and celebrate that you are special, even sacred, just the way you are. If you choose not to drive for that one day, you may realize how few of your friends are in walking distance and consider getting to know your neighbors a bit better. Or try finding a way to show your kids you love them without taking them to a store to buy them something. You may be surprised by what you learn about your family.

Because we are still entrenched in the model of authoritative commandment, Sabbath feels to most modern Jews like an obligation—like more work. We pity the poor Orthodox Jews who aren't allowed to turn on a light switch or hop in the car. Instead of taking the day "off," they walk to the synagogue and chant in Hebrew. But their choice of how to celebrate Sabbath need not be ours. As the authors of our own *halakhah*, we can investigate the core values of Shabbat as described by our best texts and thinkers and then devise an experience of *kadosh* that is most meaningful to us today.

Some associates of mine at *Adbusters* magazine, a stridently anticonsumerist publication out of Canada, have instituted an annual "buy-nothing day," during which they encourage everyone to refrain from shopping. When I showed some of *Adbusters'* materials to an Orthodox rabbi I was interviewing for this book, he shrugged and said sadly, "But they don't know where it came from."

Rather than celebrating the extension of *halakhah* into the secular affairs of non-Jews—the innovations of Sabbath and the sabbatical are Judaism's most widely accepted gifts to Western civilization—he bemoaned the bastardization of Jewish law and its assimilation into a culture that had no awareness of its origins. Where is the shame in this? That we have lost our exclusive hold over the Sabbath or that we have lost the credit for its invention? The adaptation of the spirit of *halakhah* by Jews who choose to interpret its reasoning for themselves is Judaism at its best. Encouraging the adoption of *halakhah*'s core values by non-Jews who revive it in a completely secular context is not against our religion at all—it is Judaism's greatest blessing.

REINVENTING RITUAL

Jewish ritual life provides us with an even broader palette of alternatives for practice. We more readily understand that our rituals have been devised for our betterment, rather than for God's, which is why we can take their performance a little less seriously. Unlike *halakhah,* which stands as a universally applicable ethical template, rituals serve more to distinguish our community. They're what make us *us.*

Rituals generally have three main functions in a society. Magical rituals are conducted for the purpose of affecting nature. A certain dance might be thought to make the clouds release rain, or it is hoped that the placement of a talisman will ward off an evil spirit. Sacramental rituals are performed in order to provide focus or create an inner state. They are meant to change the person performing the ritual. The Holy Communion is a sacrament in which a wafer and wine, under the right conditions, transubstantiate within the believer into the body and blood of Christ. Although its execution involves a supernatural event, the ritual is performed not to create a magical result, but to purify or redeem the doer. Like the sacrifices that Jews once performed in the Holy Temple, sacramental rituals must be carried out by special people under special circumstances. Without an ordained priest, transubstantiation will not take place. Similarly, the Jewish God would only accept a sacrifice if the *cohanim* were present to offer it. Both magical and sacramental rituals seem inappropriate for a people who shun superstition and who believe that neither God nor nature can be compelled to behave in a certain way.

The third style of ritual—the one that best applies to Jews today—takes place in a more figurative context. This type of ritual is more like theater or a visit to a museum. We don't believe anything magical is actually taking place or that anything tangible—like rain or peace—will result from the ceremony. It is more of a reenactment carried out to keep something in our sense memory. Unlike audience members or book readers, participants in rituals can engage, as actors, in a performance that has symbolic meaning and sensorial components. It is a form of play that extends a common language throughout a community. All practicing Jews know what, say, *haroseth* is (a mixture of apples, nuts, and wine used during the Passover seder), which gives us a shared set of experiences from which to relate to one another. (Didn't you feel like an insider for knowing what *haroseth* is—or an outsider for not knowing?) Rituals form the fabric of Jewish life and let us feel "at home" wherever other Jews might be.

On Purim, for example, we do more than simply read the story of Esther out loud in the synagogue. We dress up in costumes and perform in a pageant. We twirl the *gregor* (noisemaker) whenever we hear the name of our nemesis, Haman. We drink until we can no longer make out the words on the page. These rituals give us sensory access to the stories we tell, a way of remembering these experiences with our bodies, and a way to bring our religion into the realm of play. This is why we can still remember the holidays we celebrated as children.

Rituals let us experience our myths as more than stories on a page. But they also ensure we experience them as anything but *real*. The Purim ritual brings the essence of *hineni* to the story of Esther. *Here I am, reenacting the biblical legend.* No one actually believes he or she is Mordechai or Esther. It is not some form of voodoo possession. Quite the contrary, it is *less* hypnotic than watching a play or a movie. We are backstage and onstage in the re-creation of the story. We are all the more conscious of the artifice. Ironically, our participation gives us more distance from the reality of the story we are performing. We are rendered more capable of interpreting the narrative critically and applying its themes to our contemporary experience. Rituals create dimensional context.

Jews who are aware of the religion's clear rejection of sorcery and magical thinking often shy away from rituals that seem to betray a superstitious mind-set. No thinking Jew wants to put a mezuzah on his doorpost if the only justification he knows of is to ward off evil spirits. To do so reminds us of how *un*-Jewish we are every time we see it. But at the same time, we yearn to be connected to our faith in a way that involves some of the customs that have for centuries distinguished us as a people.

Luckily, there are many ways to engage in rituals in a manner that augments our own connection to their meaning. One such path is study. Too often we celebrate Jewish holidays with no real knowledge of their true history or context. We might remember stray details from the religious instruction of our childhoods, but even these, we suspect, are most likely candy-coated interpretations by ethnic apologists. One way to revital-ize any ritual would be to research the true history of the holiday it celebrates. The facts uncovered in such a search are occa-sionally disillusioning, but, in the end, the truth is often the key to setting these holidays free.

The festival of Purim is still loaded with imagery from its earlier incarnation as a fertility myth of the male god Marduk and Ishtar, the virgin warrior. The *hamantaschen,* a triangular holiday pastry, is iconic for the female anatomy and covered with poppy seeds, another symbol of fertility. Even the name of the story's antagonist, Haman, many scholars believe, comes from the same root as the word *hymen*—an obstacle to fertilization.

Today's fledgling efforts at Jewish reinvention take the origins of Purim at face value. I've attended modern Purim reenactments that highlight the fertility myths on which the holiday is based, with no effort at discovering what eventually attracted rabbis to turn it into part of the Jewish canon. With the best of intentions, the organizers of these events create stunning pageants but go so far back into the holiday's origin that they offer us only the pagan sensibilities out of which the Jewish holiday was developed.

A more constructive but research-intensive strategy might be to focus on how the holiday was changed as it was incorporated into Judaism. By locating the translations that were made in the myth and ritual, we can discover what it is that makes this holiday quintessentially Jewish. Of course, the key difference is that the imbalance in Purim is not solely between mythic sexual energies, but also between a king and his people. By deferring his responsibilities to a tyrannical prime minister, the king has recklessly endangered the integrity of his throne. Because Mordechai refuses to bow to Haman, all Jews are to be executed. When Ishtar intervened in the original story, she saved her followers from death. When Esther—a fully assimilated Persian—intervenes selflessly on behalf of the Jews, she must risk her own life by exposing and reclaiming her own Jewishness.

The Purim ritual offers plenty of opportunity to highlight the elements of the story that exemplify its particularly Jewish emphasis on social justice, the danger of tyranny, and the need to reclaim one's Jewishness in light of the threat to others. By delving deep into the story's origins rather than shying away from them, we can connect more directly to its mythic core and its feminist shadings.

Hanukkah, the Jewish Festival of Light, is usually recounted as the story of how the Maccabees, the first generation of the Hasmonaean Jewish dynasty, fought to reclaim the Holy Temple from the anti-Semitic Greeks. After the Maccabees won the war, we are told, they came upon a tiny amount of oil in the Holy Temple lamp, but it miraculously lasted for eight days.

We don't have access to the Hanukkah story in official Jewish literature. The books of the Maccabees were not included in the final version of the Jewish Bible—most likely because the tale they tell doesn't reflect too well on the Jews as we sometimes like to see ourselves. We don't generally celebrate military victories as religious holidays anyway. By consulting the Catholic Bible's Apocrypha (a collection of biblical books that didn't make the Jews' final cut), or any good history of the period, we learn that the Maccabean conflicts were largely a civil war.

Israel had been under Greek control since Alexander the Great. Although the Greeks first tolerated the local religions of the people in their provinces, the threat of Roman invasion encouraged less enlightened leaders, like Antiochus IV, to institute a state religion. He campaigned hard to assimilate the Jews. By the second century B.C.E., most Jews had already surrendered to the Hellenist way of life, even before certain Jewish rituals were declared illegal. The Jewish priests were themselves collaborators, having traded in their sacrificial duties for nude wrestling in a gymnasium built next to the Temple. This led to a new emphasis on Greek ideals such as the perfection of the body and encouraged many Jews to spurn circumcision, which they began to see as the desecration of one of God's perfect creations. Many Jews hid their circumcisions, and some even sought to reverse them through primitive surgery and other painful methods.

The Hasmonaeans were a fundamentalist minority from the hinterlands, who had been watching their decadent urban counterparts in Jerusalem with horror for over a century. But the voluntary reversal of circumcision was the last straw. The Hasmonaeans were totalitarian in their own right, believing that all aspects of life must be dictated by the Torah. Their struggle was not against the Greeks, it was against the assimilated Jews, whose altars they destroyed and on whom they performed forced circumcisions. Vigilante groups pushed priests back into their original roles in the Temple until there was enough official Jewish support for a revolt.

When it was over, the Maccabees forced the male inhabitants of Jerusalem to undergo circumcision. (Flush with victory, they forced circumcision on the inhabitants of several nearby non-Jewish cities as well.) They made themselves both the high priests and the monarchs of Israel, supplanting the Davidic line. As a result, most Jews saw the Hasmonaean refusal to submit to Greek culture and religion as a political struggle, with nationalist overtones. In truth, the war was not so much a rebellion against totalitarianism or anti-Semitism as a revolt against the Jews' own waning support for circumcision. The Hasmonaeans themselves became pro-Hellenist just a few decades later, their reign finally ending with King Herod.

The Hanukkah story was later revised by the Pharisees and the writers of the Talmud, who were contending with Greek and Roman problems of their own. The miracles of the oil lamp was invented, and the holiday became the "Festival of Light," in the spirit of earlier solstice rituals. It was considered a fairly minor holiday, rising in stature only as we have come to live among Christians and felt the need to celebrate something as splendid as Christmas.

How are we to approach such a historically difficult holiday in a way that is meaningful for us today? We might try starting from today's truth. We all know what it is like to live in a country where we can't really participate in the biggest holiday of the year, and many of us have the sense that the Hanukkah of "eight nights of gifts" is a cobbled-together substitute for its Christian counterpart. Many of us feel somewhat left out of what the rest of our country is celebrating. But, however assimilated we are, for many of us—like my dot-com friend Eric—to bring a Christmas tree into our homes crosses a kind of line. Assimilation to American culture was supposed to mean pluralism, not the assumption of Christianity.

In this context, the performance of Hanukkah today recapitulates the historical event on which it was based. The Maccabees, though staunch and violent fundamentalists, were fighting for the right to maintain a unique religious identity. Antiochus had offered the Jews complete equality, if only they would adopt the Greek way. How many of you have friends who simply don't understand why you won't celebrate Christmas? They probably tell you that it isn't really a religious holiday and that you should simply give in. Still, some of us can't or won't.

The celebration of Hanukkah is another assertion of our distinctiveness in the face of the forces of assimilation. We may accept that we live in a largely Christian culture but won't go so far as to celebrate the birth of their Messiah. It just goes against our grain. By placing a menorah in the window, we join in the spirit of seasonal holidays in our own way, while remembering a much graver historical confrontation with the same basic issues.

This suggests yet another way of approaching Jewish ritual. As leaders of our own ceremonies, particularly in the home, we have the authority to update them however we choose so they make more sense to us and our families—as long as we base our decisions on our best efforts to understand the ritual's intended effects in its original context. We can analyze a ritual, decide what it means to us today, and then adapt it or add to it in a way that reflects these values.

Let's take as one example the ritualistic remembrance of the ten plagues, as performed during the Passover seder. We've already seen how the plagues don't represent attacks by God on the Egyptians as much as the desecration of the idols that the Israelites most likely worshiped themselves, before they came to accept the Jewish concept of God. During the seder, we spill a tiny amount of wine as we recite the name of each of our former icons—almost as if we are acknowledging the pain of letting go of these once familiar, if idolatrous, comforts. What if, for instance, we extended that ritual by asking each person at the table to spill one more drop of wine while saying, out loud, the name of a current idol from which they're willing to be liberated? Money? Power? Fame? Fashion? A famous rock star? This modified plagues ritual serves to recontextualize any idol of our choosing as a plague. We restore the ancient ritual with the power to aid us in our current emotional and spiritual challenges.

Because we would have taken it upon ourselves to research the origins of the Haggadah, we would also know that much of the seder ritual was devised during the Bar Kokhba revolt against the Roman occupation. The "Egyptians" we speak of were understood, centuries ago, to be a code word for the oppressive Romans. For example, the famous line from the Haggadah, "A wandering Aramean was my father," more accurately translates to "The Romans sought to destroy my patrimony."

How are we oppressed today, and how can we represent this at a seder? One answer comes in the form of a ritual inspired by the feminist struggle. A rabbi was once asked about the place of women in Jewish leadership. He is reported to have responded, "A woman has as much place at the pulpit as an orange does on a seder plate." And so the tradition of placing an orange on the seder plate was born. It is an act of defiance—a ritualistic iconoclasm in the spirit of the original Passover sacrifice. It disrupts the seemingly inviolable sanctity of a seder plate, with its predetermined partitions, in order to promote the agenda of the currently oppressed.

Another way to imbue old rituals with current meaning is to respond to the words and actions honestly and then pursue these reactions as far and as deeply as possible. Again, it's necessary to have some research on the ritual being practiced.

For example, Irwin Kula, a progressive rabbi and scholar, was once asked to serve as the guest rabbi on the pulpit of a large New Jersey synagogue on Yom Kippur. The time came to recite a prayer known as the *Unetaneh tokef* ("You should give us strength"), from an eleventh-century poem about God's mythical *Book of Life and Death.* "On Rosh Hashanah it is written and on Yom Kippur it is sealed," we recite, "who shall live and who shall die." God has already decided which good and bad things are going to happen to us, and there's not a lot we can do about it. It's a somewhat severe concept for Jews, who resist all notions of preordination. Even the poem's assertion that "repentance, prayer, or righteousness" can help one to transcend or "cross over" these perils offers little consolation to modern people who cherish free will and mastery over their own fate.

As Kula watched the congregation recite the prayer, he realized they were losing steam. He could tell they weren't connecting with its meaning or its implications. So he stopped them in the middle and asked if anyone believed what they were reciting. Almost none did.

In the ensuing discussion, the congregants shared their misgivings about the poem. One man, a recent widower, was particularly disturbed by the notion that God would have decided to take his two sons' mother from them.

Kula and the congregation took the next half hour to analyze the poem together. The surface way of understanding the poem is that God is in control of our destiny. But does a closer look at the poetry show anything else? One congregant noticed that the order of good and bad possibilities was not symmetrical. Contrary to what we might expect, the poem doesn't list one's possible fates in a rhythmic alternation of life or death, rich or impoverished, healthy or sick, but mixes them up. There is no order.

The congregation decided that the poet may have been more intelligent and subversive than they first suspected. What if the random order of these fates meant to show there is no pattern—no design—in the mishaps or good fortunes that befall us? Maybe they just happen.

Kula backed up their conclusion with a bit of biblical commentary. The words of the poem are drawn from two books of the Bible: Esther, the one book where God does not appear;

and Ecclesiastes, which says that it's all in vain—good people sometimes die young, and the wicked often live a long time. So, with a little analysis, the prayer says something quite different beneath the surface: Our fates are quite random and out of our control. God is not even present.

As the conversation developed, the widower explained that the only reason he came to synagogue that day was to visit with "that family in the next row." He'd been sitting behind them for ten years. "They took care of us a lot this year, and I wanted to see them."

When the congregation returned to the prayer, nobody missed its meaning in this new context: You can't control whether you live or die, but you can control whether you still care about people. You won't avert the evil decree— but you can avert what the poem calls the *roah,* or bitterness, of the decree. We love and support one another, despite the randomness.

The congregation redeemed the prayer by opening it up to what people really believed. It takes a certain fearlessness and a faith that the text will eventually offer up an alternative. But even failure is better than continuing to worship God in a way that has already died.

RUN TO THE *BEIT MIDRASH*

I was at a Hanukkah party a few years ago that happened to fall on a Friday night, Sabbath. None of us were rabbis, and a discussion broke out about whether the Hanukkah or the Shabbat candles should be lit first.

"Shabbat is the more important holiday," one woman argued. "So we should do that first."

"If it's more important," chimed in a young dancer, "then it should go last. Like in a curtain call."

We finally decided that since the Shabbat candles mark Sabbath evening, after which no more work is to be done or candles lit, we'd have to light the Hanukkah candles first. Then we'd light the Sabbath candles and then get on with the party. No, none of us observed the Sabbath, at least not in any strict no-lights-or-cars way. That wasn't the point. We wanted to do one thing "right" and took tremendous delight in ascertaining what that correct action would be, given our rather limited knowledge of Jewish law and lore. (It turns out we were right about the order.)

Our methodology made us feel like talmudic sages. But we weren't. Our Jewish educations had been pitiful, and the wealth of our collective historical and theological data was very thin. Yes, we had engaged in the style of community discussion for which our tradition is famous, but we didn't really have the wealth of knowledge that makes such a discussion very meaningful. The spirit was willing, but the knowledge was weak.

Although a participatory and self-authored relationship to Judaism will be key to its survival in the coming years, our rejection of the religion's obsolete institutions needn't rob us of the ability to educate ourselves. In the late 1970s, responding to their congregations' waning interest in Judaism, many synagogues expanded their educational offerings and changed their Saturday morning services to include *d'var Torah* (Torah discussion), led by the rabbi. Unfortunately, most of these efforts emphasized the agendas of the religious institutions and the assimilation-fearing federations that funded them. Torah passages and synagogue liturgy were analyzed in light of their ability to stem the tide of intermarriage and assimilation. Rarely did Jewish education expose congregants to the political, religious, or cultural influences informing the Torah narratives, and even more rarely did it offer a working knowledge of the tools we might use to analyze and criticize Torah for ourselves.

Although most synagogues today still offer very little deep instruction in Torah and Jewish history, there was a time when this was their principal function. Perhaps this role should be restored or replaced by something new—or even replaced by something very old.

The *beit midrash,* "house of study," was developed in the Second Temple period as a component of the synagogue.

While the function of synagogue was to offer an opportunity for community worship beyond centralized Temple rites, the *beit midrash* was dedicated exclusively to the study of text. The synagogue liturgy was really just a substitute for sacrifices. The *beit midrash* gave Jews and, eventually, non-Jews alike direct access to the original source material informing the mythology, *halakhah,* rituals, and worldview that constitute Judaism. The talmudic sages stressed that Torah study takes precedence over synagogue worship, going so far as to say that "if you are new to a town and learn of a synagogue, walk there. If you learn there is a *beit midrash,* run."

This emphasis held for quite some time, and although the Yiddish word *shul* actually means "school," the unique role of the *beit midrash* was eventually subordinated to that of the sanctuary. By the modern era, *beit midrash* came to mean the library attached to the synagogue, where the most motivated members could seek out the resources they needed for independent study. As Jews lost direct access to Torah and grew increasingly disconnected from the spirit of inquiry, services became more about creating mood than inspiring the quest for knowledge and sense. Well-meaning rabbis were forced to fit morsels of Jewish education into their sermons, which took on the tone of moralizing homilies rather than points of intellectual or spiritual departure. People began to think of the synagogue as a place to hear answers instead of a place to find new questions.

In order to fuel a renaissance in participatory Judaism, we will need to reverse this trend and reinvent a *beit midrash* for our age. If everyone's point of view is to matter, then everyone must be given the basic tools they need to generate an informed opinion. Although the private study of sacred texts and their commentaries can take a person a long way, part of the Jewish mandate is to wrestle not just with Torah, but with one another. There is no such thing as personal revelation or individual enlightenment in Judaism. Unlike the Gnostic and mystical traditions, Judaism does not offer transcendence from the real world or the body through spiritual practice. The Torah's few references to resurrection always involve taking the body along, too. This is meant not to promote materialism or a fixation on the sensual, but to maintain Judaism's emphasis on life—this life, *real* life—as the locus of our concern. Study must not be a retreat from community, but a way to forge one.

Much more challenging than monasticism, which doesn't exist as an option in Judaism, is the journey toward group enlightenment through forging a dynamic pluralism, even when it must simultaneously support contradictory beliefs. Jewish education occurs through dialogue; our institutions are safe havens where honest, penetrating, and even gut-wrenchingly disillusioning discussions must be allowed to flower.

The *beit midrash* model is akin to that of a teaching hospital: to learn is to teach, and to teach is to learn. This is why medical centers with an emphasis on education also offer the most cutting-edge treatments for disease. Students asking questions keep experienced surgeons on their toes, aware of new techniques and medical breakthroughs, and lead them to consider alternatives to their established practices. It's a harder job for the respected surgeon, no doubt, but one that enriches everyone involved.

The job of a new *beit midrash* would be to give all seekers direct access to Torah—the very source code of Judaism—as well as a place to hash out their interpretations. By direct access, I don't mean simply to the text itself, but also to the many myths, historical events, and literary conventions that went into its creation. In order to understand Torah, we must learn to hear its stories and laws as they were heard by the people for whom it was written. Although its teachings may be regarded as timeless, the creation and redacting of the Torah text occurred at certain moments in history, with very specific considerations in mind. So, too, did the countless efforts at interpreting it over the ages. For a genuine renaissance in Judaism to occur, we must get ourselves as close to the Torah's original forms as possible so they can be reborn in our new context.

This strategy contradicts a long-supported talmudic instruction for each new generation to begin its inquiry into

Torah wherever the last generation left off. The talmudic sages didn't want centuries of successive insights to be discarded casually by the uninformed reader. But the current Jewish condition, our disconnection from text and one another, and our quite misdirected notions of race and national identity may require us to go a bit further back than our sages suggested. It's not about rejecting the rabbis; its about not having to experience religion entirely through the footnotes of others. How far back must we go to reorient ourselves to Judaism's essential codes? As far back as necessary to make the Jewish model fit our current reality, but no further back than the Torah itself. For Jews, the Torah is the point of origin. While we can allow our performance of *halakhah* to be dictated by the incremental adjustments of our evolving community ethical template, meaningful literary criticism requires us to wrestle with the source material, with as much knowledge as we can attain of the conditions under which it was first created and understood.

The Torah's ancient audience understood its references and jokes much in the same way a modern audience might understand the references in a popular song or an episode of their favorite television show. How could a listener with no awareness of our social context ever be expected to glean that Paul Simon's "Kodachrome" is a satire of middle-class values rather than an ode to a Nikon camera? No more than a modern reader could be expected to know that Jacob's sons in the Torah—Judah, Benjamin, Reuben, and so on—were understood as being not real people, but mythical characters, each one representing an entire, well-known tribe. (If we did, imagine how much less distracted we would be by the whole notion of a Jewish "bloodline.") Their behaviors as characters mirror, and sometimes satirize, the then well-known history of the tribe. We simply cannot be expected to resonate with the structure and meaning of our Torah unless we learn how to read it as it was first read.

Indeed, a great majority of the Torah is incomprehensible without a working knowledge of the customs and beliefs of the Israelites or the religious practices of the many neighbors from whom they were attempting to distinguish themselves. Successive efforts at interpretation were themselves conceived in very specific social and political contexts. By using them to translate Torah for us, we end up even more distant from whatever universal values the Torah may have been trying to impart. We surrender the universal to a particular that we don't understand any better.

One of my favorite Torah teachers, Rabbi Seth Frisch of the School of Divinity at Moravian College, is endlessly fascinated by the way the text comes to life once it is analyzed in its proper historical context. For example, most of us understand the *aquedah,* the story of Abraham's binding of Isaac, as evidence of our patriarch's heroically unselfish devotion to God. Abraham loved his son dearly, we are told by our rabbis and a majority of interpreters, but when commanded by God to sacrifice Isaac upon an altar, he went against all the instincts in his body. With great sorrow he walked his son up to the altar, bound him, and raised a knife to slay him. Suddenly, from out of nowhere, an angel of mercy spared Abraham from this terrifying trial. He breathed a great sigh of relief and was informed that this was only a "test" by God to see if Abraham really loved his God enough to sacrifice his dearest son.

As Frisch has concluded, the text in its original context refutes this interpretation quite clearly. Today's misreading of the *aquedah* was first developed around the time of the Crusades, when Jews had once again resorted to sacrificing their own children rather than letting them be abducted by the Crusaders, who might torture them, kill them, or force their conversion. The Torah story was twisted to help the persecuted Jews rationalize the painful choice they were making in a time of terrible violence and uncertainty. Whether this was the appropriate course for the Torah's interpreters to take is for history to judge. The fact that it has remained our interpretation of "the *aquedah* test" to this day is our responsibility to correct.

In its original context, as we have already touched upon, Abraham's story would have been understood very differently. Abraham, on hearing his God's command, shows no signs of hesitation. It was not a test at all, in this regard, but the conventional practice. Abraham hesitates only when he is instructed by God's angel to halt the proceedings. The angel needs to tell Abraham not once, but *twice* that this sacrifice need no longer be performed. The real test of Abraham is if he has enough faith in his God to *refrain* from the standard and time-honored rite. (That Isaac was not Abraham's first son at all, but his second, adds even more layers of meaning about the relationship of Israel to Egypt that ancient audiences would have immediately understood.)

The *aquedah* provides us with just one example of how we have actually reversed the meaning of Torah through our inability to interpret the text for ourselves. And it is one of the most central myths of our religion! Making matters worse, the current structure of synagogue worship prevents rabbis from correcting the situation. When I presented this new interpretation of the *aquedah* to a Reform rabbi in Florida for his thoughts, the man broke down and cried. I asked him why.

"Because each year on Rosh Hashanah, when we read that portion of the Torah, I give a sermon that says the reverse. What else can I do? How do you think they'd react if I told them Abraham wanted to sacrifice his son or that the Torah was meant to abolish our practice of killing children? They didn't hire me to tell them this."

We can't handle the truth. Or so our rabbis fear—which is why it is not up to them to change the way that synagogue obstructs instead of enhances our relationship to Torah. It is up to us.

The Jewish people were led first by priests, then by rabbis, and then by the philanthropies that we funded to preserve our faith through the difficult transition into the modern era. Now it is up to us, the Jewish people, to create or refashion institutions capable of fostering the kinds of conversations that will give us the knowledge and agency required to wrestle with our own texts together.

The Conservative movement has already taken a first step toward this end by publishing a new translation of the Torah, complete with critical essays that challenge the historical integrity of Jewish mythology. One essay reveals how the Noah story was based on a legend from Mesopotamia. Another shows how a mass exodus of Hebrews from Egypt never actually occurred. Publications including *The New York Times* applauded the effort as a unique breakthrough in the relationship of Jews to their texts. What these reviewers failed to realize, though, was that the ancients—not to mention Ezra, Maimonides, and Spinoza—already regarded the Torah as allegory. Our emerging historical understanding of our mythology is the exception, not the rule.

By releasing the Torah from its obligation to serve as a historical record, we liberate it, and ourselves, to generate an unending bounty of narratives through which to create meaning.

NEGOTIATING OUR TRUTH

All narratives are not equal. Striving toward a universal and multifaceted collective story requires judgment and negotiation, not just the tolerant acceptance of every idea that comes along. By educating ourselves about Torah and its history, we gain the critical faculties required to make informed decisions. By engaging with one another in the pursuit of a shared sensibility about our relationship to the gift of life, we come to engender the very spirit of Jewish community. Study and the sharing of insights are the vehicles through which we learn to live together in a meaningful way.

What makes this so challenging is that it is not a free-for-all. Although we have no top-down authority to direct our inquiry—many of us don't even believe in God—we nonetheless have the means to create the conditions through which a genuinely applicable ethical template can emerge. We must not be so desperate for renaissance, however, that we accept that every effort at redefining Judaism is as valuable as every other.

Our hunger for a renewed relationship to faith has led many to rush to well-packaged solutions that either lack any connection to Judaism's source code or conflict directly with it. Recently I was called into a meeting to advise a gentleman who claimed to have received the funding necessary to launch a

Jewish television channel. He thought that the effort could help centralize the focus of the disparate Jewish people by providing them with a regular broadcast that reflected their values. But whose values? Would he show reruns of *Seinfeld* followed by evening services? Which services? Reform? Far from his consciousness was the fact that Judaism has not had any centralized authority since the destruction of the Second Temple in 70 C.E. Would a Jewish TV channel mean to serve that function? At the very least, these questions need to be asked.

On other occasions, I have been invited to "Jewish" rituals based on one or another of the pagan rites that first informed them or on the spontaneous contributions of the painfully uninformed congregations in attendance. Had the creators of these rituals bothered to do the meticulous research required of those who would reinvent rituals, or sought to educate their audiences rather than simply entertaining them, their events might have been a more valuable experience for the hundreds of children in attendance. Instead of subjecting the proceedings to critical review, their sponsors applauded them merely for getting a bunch of Jews into a synagogue on Friday night.

Others are busy creating glossy magazines, hip Web sites, and speed-dating services to answer the need of modern Jews to relate to their religion in a different way. Rather than rewarding such efforts simply because they are nominally Jewish (At last! Someone young cares about Judaism!), we must regard them as critically as we judge anything else. Do they make us question? Do they increase our understanding of Judaism? Or are they merely new ways of distancing us from the source of our beliefs? Do they instill us with new avenues for meaningful inquiry, or do they discredit the secular path even further through their unintentionally misinformed messages?

The enthusiastic promotion of all things calling themselves "Jewish" is a form of idolatry as dangerous as any other—perhaps more dangerous, because Judaism is the very faith almost solely dedicated to eradicating such orientations. In Judaism, nothing is sacred—at least not anything that you or I are capable of producing or even conceiving.

This is why we must engage one another. Keep one another honest. Educate one another to the best of our ability, cling to the facts we do have until they are convincingly disproved, and argue forcefully for what we believe in. This process is the responsibility and privilege of people who would strive to be Jewish, whether or not they call it Judaism at all. For even this word can become a sacred cow to those who use it to confirm their moral or racial superiority. We must engage with all comers if we ever hope to transcend our own fundamentalism and live in a world where social justice becomes a universal priority.

The Jewish contention that nothing is sacred means more than rejecting all forms of idolatry. By confirming our iconoclasm at every turn, we create the space for something sacred to emerge between us. Judaism, our texts, and our practices are all designed to create a kind of emptiness. It is not the emptiness of despair or the loss of meaning. It is the emptiness that mythic Abraham felt on being denied the right to sacrifice his son. It is the emptiness of the holy "tent of meeting" that the Israelites carried through the desert that held place for a new kind of God that had no idol. It is this emptiness, this nothingness itself, that holds open the possibility for the divine to emerge.

This nothing is sacred.

NOW WHAT?

I REALIZE THAT MANY JEWS TODAY, myself included, are confronting some very challenging questions about the role that spirituality, religion, and Judaism itself should play in our lives. And I understand that this book, in many ways, poses more questions than it answers.

For most of us, it takes a major life event to bring our relationship to Judaism to the fore: we get married, we have a child, or maybe a parent dies. Suddenly, our new situation demands that we consider how we will incorporate our Jewishness, if at all. How "Jewish" should our wedding be? Is it okay to intermarry? Should someone convert? How "Jewish" should we raise our kids? What counts as raising them "Jewish," anyway? When someone dies, may we turn to the comfort of Jewish ritual even if we ignore it the rest of the time? Is it hypocritical to practice only the parts of Judaism we like, or only on special occasions? Or only when we *need* it?

Politics can also quite suddenly challenge our Jewish identity, as it forces us to consider our relationship to Israel. How are we to react to crises in the Middle East, as people and as Jews? Do we defend Israel's right to exist when debating with anti-Semites, but criticize Israeli policies when among Zionist extremists? Should we support Israel as our people's homeland or reject its theocratic style of governance? Can we do both?

If we do decide to pursue a specifically Jewish path, exactly how should we go about it? Can we belong to a movement and synagogue without agreeing entirely with the tenets they espouse? Does a synagogue even exist that teaches Judaism as we would want our children to practice it? Or should we forgo organized Judaism in favor of home-style meetings on Shabbat afternoon, where we can struggle together, as laypeople, with that week's Torah portion? Can we just practice social justice and not worry about all of the ritual, prayer, and study?

Different groups and individuals will surely evolve different right answers. The tradition teaches, quite emphatically, that the challenge of Judaism—like any other challenge—should be approached with questions, intelligence, knowledge, open-mindedness, and as many other questioning, intelligent, knowledgeable, and open-minded people as we can find. It is a difficult process with no easy answers. Any answers usually come with more questions of their own, anyway.

Whichever parts of Judaism or its style of inquiry we may choose to practice, my sense is that these questions of "How much is enough?" or "How Jewish must I be?" are a distraction from the matter at hand. I'd like to think that Judaism has a greater purpose than merely facilitating each person's individual reconciliation with Jewishness. Judaism surely doesn't exist for its own sake. True enough, our duty to memory and ingrained sense of obligation has probably helped to sustain Judaism—even among people who did not understand it—over the darker periods in our history. Rituals, even conducted in blind obedience, can still manage to preserve and transmit some of their meaning to future generations.

But I don't believe we are in such a dark age or that today's population of Jews need content themselves with being mere carriers of a faith they don't understand. Instead, as thinking adults, we should evaluate the relevancy and meaningfulness of our Jewishness based on its ability to bring us a sense of clarity, to help us be better people, or to enable us to actualize something beneficial to the real world, in this life. Or, using Hillel's yardstick, we should engage with our Jewishness to the extent that it keeps things from being done to other people that we wouldn't want done to ourselves.

In this sense, Jewish continuity has little to do with

whether people continue to call themselves Jewish. Real continuity of the Jewish project can only be measured in how much of the world acts as if what they do matters, on this plane and any other. If this book might serve any greater purpose, it would be to help others argue this point to friends and family who see such a stance as the abandonment of one's Jewishness.

Whether or not anyone decides to delve deeper into Judaism after reading this book—and this was not my intent—Judaism does provide us with some mechanisms for attacking the larger challenges in our spiritual and ethical lives. We are probably serving the tradition of Judiasm best when we worry less about the degree to which we meet the obligation we have to Judaism and, instead, consider the obligation we have, as Jews, to the entire world. Judaism is a means toward bringing more mindfulness, compassion, and justice into the lives of real people. There is nothing sacred for us to worry about except one another.

Above all, we must not mistake our personal challenges with Judaism for the deeper imperative at its core: engaging in the difficult work of making the most ethical, compassionate, life-affirming choice in every situation. The best reason I can think of to pursue Judaism's texts, teachings, and dialogues is to figure out what those choices are and how to muster the courage and resolve to live them.

To life.

B'SHEM OMRO: "IN THE NAME OF THE PERSON WHO SAID IT"

SINCE TALMUDIC TIMES, it has been the obligation of Jewish commentators to acknowledge the sources of their ideas. To fail in this regard is considered a sin, while to make a statement in the name of its originator is thought to "bring redemption to the world."

While these brief sections on sources for further research may fall short of redeeming the world, I hope they at least partly redeem my tremendous debt to the many scholars, authors, rabbis, and kind friends upon whose thinking so much of this book is based. They should also provide you with a brief guide to the resources to which you might choose to turn for more information and alternative insights into the issues I've raised.

One: The Transparent Faith

The evolution of the Jewish religion described in this chapter was informed largely by Karen Armstrong's *A History of God*. While I used many other sources in constructing my narrative of the development of abstract monotheism, Armstrong's straightforward analysis and uncolored, even-handed chronicle of the formations of the Jewish, Islamic, and Christian faiths provided me with a point of reference against which to compare the ideas and assertions of others. Her book is an indispensable reference to the period.

Another fine source for studying the evolution of abstract monotheism is *God: A Biography* by Jack Miles, which offers a thought-provoking character study of God through a series of close readings and literary analysis of the Bible.

For general reference to the history of the Hebrews, Israelites, and Jews, you should make use of the *Encyclopedia Judaica,* an authoritative compendium on all areas of Jewish history, custom, and theology, available in most libraries as a bound set and also in an abridged version and a CD-ROM at more reasonable prices for home use. You might also peruse H. H. Ben Sasson's extraordinarily well-researched *A History of the Jewish People* for a comprehensive, unsentimental, and ideology-free chronicle, from prehistory through the Diaspora. Another good source for exploring what is distinct about Judaism is Abba Hillel Silver's *Where Judaism Differs.*

I've chosen the Jewish Publication Society's *Tanakh* as the default translation of the Bible quoted in this book because I find it to be the most transparent and authoritative edition available. Dr. J. H. Hertz's edition of *The Pentateuch and Haftorahs* is a wonderful explanatory resource, though, writing in the context of 1930s anti-Semitism, his commentaries are somewhat apologetic and often shy away from the more harsh realities of the Torah and Jewish history. Everett Fox's *The Five Books of Moses* is a useful secondary resource, especially for those who don't read Hebrew. Unlike the Hertz volume, Fox's poetic translation presents the darker Torah passages without evasion. For Jewish liturgy, Rabbi Nosson Scherman's *The Complete ArtScroll Siddur* provides a rather complete reference to the full Jewish prayer book, with fine literal translations and explanatory footnotes.

The tremendous involvement of Jews in social justice has been widely documented, and sources range from anecdotal evidence to census data. One good place to start is Professor Stuart Svonkin's *Jews Against Prejudice.* Focusing on American Jewish involvement in civil rights, Svonkin explains how self-preservation was expanded to an ethic of social justice and provides many concrete examples. For a broader survey of the relationship between Judaism and democracy, you might try Sandy Maisel and Ira Forman's *Jews in American Politics.*

Two: How We Lost the Plot

For more on how Jews lost the plot, take a look at Yeshayahu Leibowitz's *Judaism, Human Values, and the Jewish State.* In the book's strident but informative essays, this progressive Orthodox rabbi traces some of the many ways Jews have confused themselves about their religion's priorities and calls out, without hesitation, the people and institutions he feels are responsible. His predictions, in the early 1960s, of where extreme Zionism would lead Israel are chillingly accurate. Another way to investigate how we may have gone wrong is through the critiques of Jewish artists and activists. Jewish Women Watching (www.jewishwomenwatching.com) is an anonymous group of women activists whose pointed satires of current Jewish groups and programs have helped expose, for me, exactly where institutional and cultural Judaism derails.

To learn more about how the Jewish past might inform an evolutionary Jewish future, we can look to the insights of some of our most progressive rabbis. In a series of short essays collectively titled *Perspectives,* National Jewish Center for Learning and Leadership (CLAL) founder Irving Greenberg credits earlier periods of Jewish history with values of openness and education, demonstrating what might currently hold us back from living up to our historical potential. They should be available by contacting CLAL through their Web site at www.clal.org. I have also made use of an essay by Jonathan Sarna called "A Great Awakening," in which he chronicles what he sees as the emergent style of Jewish evolution at the turn of the twentieth century. By emphasizing a bottom-up rather than institutional, top-down approach, Sarna offers hints as to how Judaism could evolve again in our century.

For a chronicle of Judaism's decline as well as many actionable suggestions for its renewal, see Michael Lerner's passionate manifesto, *Jewish Renewal.* He has the valuable perspective of an insider to institutional Judaism, as well as the leader of an entire movement dedicated to Jewish renewal and broader issues of social justice.

For a sociological perspective on contemporary Judaism, as well as statistical information, you might try Steven Cohen and Arnold M. Eisen's *The Jew Within* or Marshall Sklare's *Observing America's Jews,* as well as the infamous "1990 National Jewish Population Survey," which can be accessed on-line on a number of sites, including www.jewish-databank.com/studies.html. For a broader look at the current state of

American civic life, Robert Wuthnow's highly anecdotal *Loose Connections* offers sociological data and arguments that suggest that rubrics of membership and official affiliation are no longer accurate ways to assess belief and involvement.

Three: A Renaissance Tradition

To read more about Exodus as revolution, you can turn to two very authoritative accounts: Aaron Wildavsky's *The Nursing Father: Moses as a Political Leader* and Michael Walzer's *Exodus and Revolution*. John Levenson's book *The Death and Resurrection of the Beloved Son* offers one of the most insightful and informative perspectives on the practice and idea of child sacrifice in the biblical era.

The Columbia History of Western Philosophy was extremely helpful for me as a background reference and timeline. For a postmodern perspective, Eugene Borowitz's survey of modern Jewish philosophy, *Choices in Modern Jewish Thought,* offers a valuable compendium, though I differ with many of his conclusions.

The reference for the relationship of Deuteronomy to Jacob's disinheritance of Reuben, as well as many similar examples of intertextual biblical readings, can be found in Calum Carmichael's *Law and Narrative in the Bible: The Evidence of the Deuteronomic Laws and the Decalogue.* See the notes for chapter 5 for more on textual criticism of Torah.

Any consideration of Judaism as a civilization, rather than simply a religion, should be informed by the work of Rabbi Mordecai Kaplan. Although I only immersed myself in his work after completing this book, I found his thinking quite resonant with the notion of a constantly evolving, open source approach to Jewish practice. His key work, *Judaism as a Civilization,* served as the foundation for the vibrant and growing Reconstructionist movement of Judaism.

My ideas about a third Jewish renaissance are informed largely by advances in math, science, and biological theory. For the Gaia hypothesis, read the classic, *Gaia: A New Look at Life on Earth* by J. E. Lovelock or Peter Russel's *The Awakening Earth: The Global Brain.* For more on how the Gaia idea affects the psychology of civilization, try Howard Bloom's *The Global Brain.* To explore the science behind new physics, take a look at David Bohm's *Wholeness and the Implicate Order* or the more accessible *The Holographic Universe* by Michael Talbot. For information on chaos math and fractals, try James Gleick's *Chaos* or, for an easier entry point, *The Turbulent Mirror* by John Briggs and F. David Peat. My own early effort, *Cyberia*, attempts to chronicle the way all these ideas trickled down from the laboratories to popular culture.

For more about the open source software movement, read Eric Raymond's book *The Cathedral and the Bazaar,* which both tells the story and outlines the principles of open source.

Four: Beyond Race and Place

To rediscover Maimonides, you might begin with Isadore Twersky's *A Maimonides Reader,* which offers representative portions of the *Mishneh Torah,* and the *Guide for the Perplexed* in one volume. You could supplement this study with David Hartman's *Maimonides: Torah and Philosophic Quest,* which details the "conflict" of philosophy and religion from a perspective that assumes their ultimate reconcilability. Leo Strauss provides an interesting bridge between Maimonides and Spinoza in his book *Spinoza's Critique of Religion.* While his ideas have proved controversial, his account is especially useful for its genealogy of religious critique, beginning with the Greeks. For historical context, biographical information, and various critical interpretations, *The Cambridge Companion to Spinoza* is a useful resource. If my book prompts you in no other direction, however, and you follow up with no other source I mention, I hope you might be inspired to encounter or reacquaint yourself with Spinoza's *Theological-Political Treatise.* A seminal exploration of individual and civic ethics, to which our contemporary ideology owes a great debt, it is also a profound meditation on freedom, much of which we have yet to fully realize.

For more on kabbalah, look to the definitive body of work produced by Gershom Scholem. His book *On the Mystical Shape of the Godhead: Basic Concepts in the Kabbalah* is a good place to start. Scholem also wrote the authoritative biography, *Sabbatai Sevi.*

For more information about emergence, start with Steven Johnson's accessible and entertaining book, *Emergence,* which successfully synthesizes and contextualizes for the layman many of the scientific and sociological insights in that important new field.

My references to Freud's argument that Judaism is an idea rather than a race come from his book *Moses and Monotheism*. Yosef Hayim Yerushalmi's *Freud's Moses* updates and refutes the facts from *Moses and Monotheism* that were subsequently disproved, while remaining faithful to many of Freud's key insights. Perhaps the best evidence of Moses' origins are to be found in the Torah itself. Moses' words are translated to the Israelites through Aaron. Although later midrashic writers invented the story of Moses acquiring a speech impediment after burning his tongue as an infant, Freud and others site his need for a translator as evidence of the fact that Moses did not speak Hebrew.

Though anti-Semitism can be approached from many angles, I largely chose the historical. James Carroll's massive effort, *Constantine's Sword: The Church and the Jews,* presents a remarkably thorough history of the Roman adoption of Christianity and the creation and development of anti-Semitism in Europe. Bernard Lewis's book *What Went Wrong?*, as well as his essays for publications such as *The New Yorker,* provide an explanation of how anti-Semitism was exported to the Arab world.

Again, I have to acknowledge my enormous debt to Karen Armstrong. Her *Battle for God* (a follow-up to *The History of God*) served as a benchmark for my research and has deeply informed my understanding of the history of religious conflict. Her analysis not only serves as a cogent admonition of the dangers of fundamentalism, but also offers insights about how and why human beings repeatedly succumb to its lure.

Arthur Hertzberg's *The Zionist Idea: A Historical Analysis and Reader* offers an informative collection of essays about all things Zionist. *The Jew in the Modern World* (edited by Mendes-Flohr and Reinharz) provides even more essays and a wide array of primary sources. Emil Fackenheim is a post-Holocaust Jewish theologian whose views of statehood, as expressed in *What Is Judaism?: An Interpretation of the Present Age,* typify the more intelligent rationale for contemporary religious Zionism. For a harsh critique of fundamentalism and religious Zionism, revisit Leibowitz's *Judaism, Human Values, and the Jewish State*.

Five: Hineni

Neil Gillman's *Sacred Fragments* was one of the most insightful books I discovered in my research. It is especially useful for understanding the impact of modernity on Jewish theology. He provides an excellent framework for appreciating the role of ritual in distinguishing a community and suggests a process through which a community can develop its own *halakhah.* Furthermore, his notes "for further study" at the end of each of his chapters inspired this appendix.

One book I found useful in defining a contemporary framework for Jewish thought is Erich Fromm's *You Shall Be As Gods.* While this text seems nearly forgotten, it should be revisited for its radical insights and its clear argument that the relationship of iconoclasm, monotheism, and social justice constitutes a truly humanist Jewish tradition.

If you'd like to tackle the Talmud, you could not do better than to begin with Montefiore and Loewe's *A Rabbinic Anthology.* Like a *Bartlett's* of the Talmud, this is a compilation of myriad important excerpts in one well-indexed volume. Making it easy to find rabbinic perspective on almost any issue, this book is often considered a sort of rabbi's "cheat sheet." It has been out of print for quite some time, however, and could prove difficult to find. Abraham Cohen's *Everyman's Talmud,* though written in the 1940s, offers another very accessible (and easier to carry) gateway to the Talmud.

Alternatively, you might want to find—and I'd think own—a copy of the outstanding *Book of Legends: Sefer Ha-Aggadah,* compiled and translated by Hebrew poet Hayim Nahman Bialik and scholarly editor Yehoshua Hana Ravnitzky. Focusing on the legends and stories of talmudic and midrashic literature, instead of the hard-core legal material, this book provides a window like none other I've found to the character of Jewish wisdom and folklore.

One of my primary sources for the background of Jewish holidays was Theodor Gaster's *Festivals of the Jewish Year,* although he unnecessarily refutes much of what I've concluded to be the true pagan underpinnings of many holidays. Heschel's *The Sabbath* is a classic text about that holiday, though more valuable for his understanding of the

Jewish sanctification of time than for what he shares about the historical origins of Shabbat. For more on the controversy surrounding Jewish rituals like circumcision, there are many resources on the World Wide Web, including "The Circumcision Information and Resource Pages" at www.cirp.org.

My own understanding of the Torah as a self-reflexive literary work was inspired by my first, and still most personally influential, Torah teacher, Rabbi Seth Frisch. Like many of today's best teachers, Rabbi Frisch favors live discussion and teaching to the publication of books. Perhaps we can convince him otherwise.

There are a few books available that teach these styles of literary inquiry, and almost of all of them have been regarded as quite revolutionary undertakings. For a great primer on applying literary criticism to the Bible, take a look at Michael Fishbane's *Biblical Text and Texture: A Literary Reading of Selected Texts.* If you have any doubts, Robert Alter's brilliant *The Art of Biblical Narrative* will convince you that a literary approach does not diminish the meaning of Torah but, rather, greatly enriches our appreciation of it. You could also consult Gerald Epstein's *Climbing Jacob's Ladder* or Harold Bloom's *Ruin the Sacred Truths,* though because these are less concerned with inspiring each reader's individual critical faculties, they tend to leave you at the mercy of their authors'.

Finally, if I may be so bold as to suggest it, you may want to look at my book *Playing the Future,* about the rise of nonlinear culture among youth. The last chapter in particular argues for how a recapitulatory spiritual sensibility emerges naturally from the hypermediated culture of young people and may be interesting to some readers because I use a Christian model to explore what this theology might look like.

Finding the Others

Unfortunately, many synagogues are ill-equipped to address the kinds of questions being raised here and the challenges arising today for concerned, thinking Jews. Most rabbis are overwhelmed by the demand for officials to preside over funerals, weddings, bar mitzvahs, and other services, as well as the pressing needs of fund-raising, administration, and congregant counseling. Though they would prefer to be available for an engaging dialogue, their resources and time are quite limited by the realities of the pulpit.

More progressive synagogues, particularly those on the West Coast and in New York, have initiated home study groups for interested congregants, often led by knowledgeable laypeople or young rabbinical interns. You can usually find out if a synagogue has such offerings by consulting their monthly bulletin or Web site. Similarly, many local colleges and seminaries with continuing education departments offer classes in Torah, Talmud, and midrash, though these settings are generally less conducive to community-based inquiry.

Jewish Community Centers vary widely in their breadth of offerings, their quality usually being more dependent on the vision of their organizers than the funding available to them. The JCC on New York's Upper West Side, for one, is blessed with an executive director who understands how a community's needs emerge from within and is always ready to meet those needs with compelling classes and programming.

For those who are looking to create their own study groups or to discuss issues of Judaism on-line in an atmosphere of open inquiry, I have prepared a Web site at www.OpenSourceJudaism.com, with a variety of user-generated discussion forums and links to other resources. I will be available there, on-line, along with any other rabbis and teachers who volunteer, to pursue any of your questions or to help you to organize a discussion group in your area.

BIBLIOGRAPHY

Alter, Robert. *The Art of Biblical Narrative.* New York: Basic Books, 1981.

Apisdorf, Shimon. *Passover Survival Kit.* Pikesville, Md.: Leviathan Press, 1994.

Armstrong, Karen. *A History of God: The 4,000-Year Quest of Judaism, Christianity, and Islam.* New York: Ballantine Books, 1993.

———. *The Battle for God.* New York: Ballantine Books, 2000.

Bakan, David. *And They Took Themselves Wives: The Emergence of Patriarchy in Western Civilization.* San Francisco: Harper & Row, 1979.

Ben-Sasson, H. H., ed. *A History of the Jewish People.* Cambridge: Harvard University Press, 1976.

Bialik, Hayim Nahman, and Yehoshua Hana Ravnitzky. *The Book of Legends: Sefer Ha-Aggadah.* New York: Schocken Books, 1992.

Bloom, Howard. *Ruin the Sacred Truths: Poetry and Belief from the Bible to the Present.* Cambridge: Harvard University Press, 1991.

Borowitz, Eugene B. *Choices in Modern Jewish Thought: A Partisan Guide.* Second Edition. West Orange, N.J.: Behram House, Inc., 1995.

Carmichael, Calum M. *Law and Narrative in the Bible: The Evidence of the Deuteronomic Laws and the Decalogue.* Ithaca: Cornell University Press, 1985.

Carroll, James. *Constantine's Sword: The Church and the Jews.* Boston: Houghton Mifflin Company, 2001.

Cohen, Abraham. *Everyman's Talmud: The Major Teachings of the Rabbinic Sages.* New York: Schocken Books, 1949.

Cohen, Shayne J. D. *The Beginnings of Jewishness: Boundaries, Varieties, Uncertainties.* Berkeley: University of California Press, 1999.

Cohen, Steven M., and Arnold M. Eisen. *The Jew Within: Self, Family, and Community in America.* Bloomington: Indiana University Press, 2000.

Eisen, Arnold M. *Rethinking Modern Judaism: Ritual, Commandment, Community.* Chicago: University of Chicago Press, 1999.

Epstein, Gerald. *Climbing Jacob's Ladder: Finding Spiritual Freedom Through the Stories of the Bible.* New York: Acmi Press, 1999.

Fackenheim, Emil L. *What Is Judaism?: An Interpretation of the Present Age.* New York: Collier Books, 1987.

Finkelstein, Norman H. *The Other 1492: Jewish Settlement in the New World.* New York: Beech Tree Books, 1989.

Fishbane, Michael. *Biblical Text and Texture: A Literary Reading of Selected Texts.* Oxford: OneWorld Publications, 1998.

Fox, Everett, trans. *The Five Books of Moses: Genesis, Exodus, Leviticus, Numbers, and Deuteronomy.* The Schocken Bible: Volume I. New York: Schocken Books, 1995.

Freud, Sigmund. *Moses and Monotheism.* New York: Random House, 1987.

_____. *Totem and Taboo: Resemblances Between the Psychic Lives of Savages and Neurotics.* A. A. Brill, trans. New York: Vintage Books, 1918.

Fromm, Erich. *You Shall Be As Gods: A Radical Reinterpretation of the Old Testament and Its Tradition.* New York: Fawcett, 1969.

Garret, Don, ed. *The Cambridge Companion to Spinoza.* Cambridge: Cambridge University Press, 1996.

Gaster, Theodor H. *Festivals of the Jewish Year: A Modern Interpretation and Guide.* New York: William Sloane Associated Publishers, 1966.

Gillman, Neil. *Sacred Fragments: Recovering Theology for the Modern Jew.* Philadelphia: Jewish Publication Society, 1990.

Goldberg, Jeffrey. "The Martyr Strategy," *The New Yorker*, (July 9, 2001).

Goldman, Ari L. *Being Jewish: The Spiritual and Cultural Practice of Judaism Today.* New York: Simon & Schuster, 2000.

Graves, Robert. *King Jesus.* New York: Farrar, Straus and Giroux, 1946.

Greenberg, Irving. *Perspectives: The Third Great Cycle of Jewish History, Voluntary Covenant, Power and Politics.* A CLAL Thesis. New York: The National Jewish Center for Learning and Leadership, 2001.

Harlow, Rabbi Jules, ed. and trans. *A Prayerbook for Shabbat, Festivals, and Weekdays.* New York: The United Synagogue of America, 1985.

Hartman, David. *Maimonides: Torah and Philosophic Quest*. New York: The Jewish Publication Society, 1976.

Hertz, Dr. J. H., ed. *The Pentateuch and Haftorahs: Hebrew Text, English Translation, and Commentary*. Second Edition. London: Soncino Press, 1960.

Hertzberg, Arthur. *The Zionist Idea: A Historical Analysis and Reader*. Philadelphia: The Jewish Publication Society, 1997.

Heschel, Abraham Joshua. *The Sabbath: Its Meaning for Modern Man*. New York: Farrar, Straus and Giroux, 1979.

Johnson, Steven. *Emergence: The Connected Lives of Ants, Brains, Cities, and Software*. New York: Scribner, 2001.

Jones, Alexander, ed. *The New Testament of the Jerusalem Bible*. Reader's Edition. New York: Image Books, 1969.

Kaplan, Mordecai. *Judaism As a Civilization: Toward a Reconstruction of American Jewish Life*. New York: Jewish Publication Society, 1981.

Leibowitz, Yeshayahu. *Judaism, Human Values, and the Jewish State*. Elizer Goldman, ed. Cambridge: Harvard University Press, 1992.

Lerner, Michael. *Jewish Renewal: A Path to Healing and Transformation*. New York: Perennial, 1995.

Levenson, John D. *The Death and Resurrection of the Beloved Son: The Transformation of Child Sacrifice in Judaism and Christianity*. New Haven: Yale University Press, 1993.

Levinas, Emmanuel. *Difficult Freedom: Essays on Judaism*. Sean Hand, trans. Baltimore: Johns Hopkins University Press, 1997.

Lewis, Bernard. *What Went Wrong?: Western Impact and Middle Eastern Response*. New York: Oxford University Press, 2002.

Maisel, L. Sandy, and Ira N. Forman. *Jews in American Politics*. New York: Rowman and Littlefield Publishers, 2001.

Mendes-Flohr, Paul, and Jehuda Reinharz. *The Jew in the Modern World: A Documentary History*. Second Edition. Oxford: Oxford University Press, 1995.

Miles, Jack. *God: A Biography*. New York: Vintage Books, 1996.

Montefiore, C. G., and H. Loewe. *A Rabbinic Anthology*. Philadelphia: The Jewish Publication Society, 1939.

Nowak, Gwen. *Miriam of Nazareth: Who Can Find Her?* Toronto: Cortleigh House, 2000.

Popkin, Richard H., ed. *The Columbia History of Western Philosophy.* New York: MJF Books, 1999.

Raymond, Eric S. *The Cathedral and the Bazaar: Musings on Linux and Open Source by an Accidental Revolutionary.* Cambridge: O'Reilly and Associates, Inc., 1999.

Rosen, Jonathan. *The Talmud and the Internet: A Journey Between Worlds.* New York: Farrar, Straus and Giroux, 2000.

Rosenzweig, Franz. *Star of Redemption.* Notre Dame: University of Notre Dame, 1971.

Ross, James R. *Fragile Branches: Travels Through the Jewish Diaspora.* New York: Riverhead Books, 2000.

Roth, Cecil, and Geoffrey Wigoder, eds. *Encyclopedia Judaica: CD-Rom Edition.* Jerusalem, Israel: Keter Publishing House Ltd., 1997.

Roth, Joseph. *The Wandering Jews: The Classic Portrait of a Vanished People.* Michael Hofmann, trans. New York: W. W. Norton and Company, 1985.

Rotjman, Betty. *Black Fire on White Fire: An Essay on Jewish Hermeneutics, from Midrash to Kabbalah.* Steven Rendall, trans. Berkeley: University of California Press, 1998.

Rushkoff, Douglas. *Playing the Future: What We Can Learn from Digital Kids.* New York: Putnam, 1999.

Sacks, Rabbi Jonathan. *A Letter in the Scroll: Understanding Our Jewish Identity and Exploring the Legacy of the World's Oldest Religion.* New York: The Free Press, 2000.

Sarna, Jonathan D. "A Great Awakening: The Transformation that Shaped Twentieth-Century American Judaism and its Implications for Today." New York: Council for Initiatives in Jewish Education, 1995.

Scherman, Rabbi Nosson, ed. and trans. *The Complete ArtScroll Siddur: Weekday, Sabbath, Festival.* New York: Mesorah Publications, Ltd., 1998.

Schiffman, Lisa. *Generation J.* San Francisco: HarperCollins, 1999.

Silver, Abba Hillel. *Where Judaism Differs: An Inquiry into the Distinctiveness of Judaism*. New York: Collier Books, 1989.

Sklare, Marshall. *Observing America's Jews*. Hanover: Brandeis University Press, 1993.

Solomon, Lewis D. *Jewish Spirituality: Revitalizing Judaism for the Twenty-first Century*. Northvale, N. J.: Jason Aronson, Inc., 2000.

Spinoza, Baruch. *Theological-Political Treatise*. Gebhard Edition. Indianapolis: Hackett Publishing Co, 2001.

Strauss, Leo. *Spinoza's Critique of Religion*. Chicago: The University of Chicago Press, 1997.

Svonkin, Stuart. *Jews Against Prejudice: American Jews and the Fight for Civil Liberties*. New York: Columbia University Press, 1997.

Tanakh, The Holy Scriptures: The New JPS Translation According to the Traditional Hebrew Text. Philadelphia: The Jewish Publication Society, 1985.

Teilhard de Chardin, Pierre. *The Future of Man*. New York: Harper & Row, 1964.

Telushkin, Rabbi Joseph. *Jewish Literacy: The Most Important Things to Know About the Jewish Religion, Its People, and Its History*. New York: William Morrow, 2001.

Twersky, Isadore, ed. *A Maimonides Reader*. New Jersey: Behram House, 1972.

Wildavsky, Aaron. *The Nursing Father: Moses as a Political Leader*. London: The University of Alabama Press, 1995.

Wine, Sherwin T. *Judaism Beyond God*. Society for Humanistic Judaism, 1995.

Wuthnow, Robert. *Loose Connections: Joining Together in America's Fragmented Communities*. Cambridge: Harvard University Press, 1998.

Yerushalmi, Yosef Hayim. *Freud's Moses: Judaism Terminable and Interminable*. New Haven: Yale University Press, 1991.

Zborowski, Mark, et al., editors, *Life Is with People: The Culture of the Shtetl*. New York: Schocken Books, 1995.

ACKNOWLEDGMENTS

THIS BOOK IS LESS A FEAT of writing than one of listening. Although it came through my keyboard, it represents the ideas, hopes, and frustrations of the hundreds of people with whom I've had the honor to converse over the past five years. In this sense, *Nothing Sacred* is as much a collaborative effort as it is an authored text. If I'm proud of anything here, it is to whatever extent I've been successful in initiating and facilitating a conversation about what it is we'd like to do about Judaism today.

I am deeply indebted to the many rabbis, teachers, and laypeople, all too numerous to mention, who shared their searches and stories with me. Still, there are some people whose contributions to this work were so profound as to require they be mentioned by name.

First and foremost is my editorial assistant, Brooke Belisle, whose tireless efforts on my behalf sustained me through numerous obstacles that appeared, at first, insurmountable. Her meticulous research and penetrating analysis of philosophical history informed the main conclusions of this work.

Roger Bennett, of The Andrea and Charles Bronfman Philanthropies, provoked me, cajoled me, and, ultimately, guided me through the perilous maze of organized Judaism. His advice to me is the same advice I'd give to anyone pursuing this subject: only engage with people and institutions that sustain you, or you'll burn out, fast.

Roger introduced me to the participants of the Reboot 2002 Summit, whose willingness to choose inquiry over certainty was as inspiring as it was informative. You were the test sample in this "open source Judaism" project and the proof that it can work. Thanks particularly to Robert Rabinowitz, Daniel Sokatch, Sharon Brous, and Amichai Lau-Lavie, who have continued to support my research with their own views and extensive learning. Thanks also to Rachel Levin, of the Righteous Persons Foundation, for her support, encouragement, and balanced perspective.

My investigation of Judaism was inspired, initially, by my friend Steven Bender, whose dissatisfaction with institutional religion led me to explore possible alternatives. The path of inquiry I chose to pursue was modeled, chiefly, on the style of textual analysis practiced by Rabbi Seth Frisch. Indeed, the "Frischian Method," as we like to call it, is unique for its unblinking dependence on what's actually being said in a particular text and the context in which it was first written.

Rabbi Andrew Bachman, of New York University, assisted and counseled me in numerous ways—most importantly, though, by exemplifying a relationship to Judaism and Jews that is honest, yet nurturing. Not an easy task. I was also aided immensely by the faculty of Clal. My conversations with the incomparably passionate Rabbi Irwin Kula led invariably to pages of new ideas, and my discussions with Rabbi Bradley Hirschfield and Dr. Shari Cohen challenged even my most progressive notions about pluralism.

I have been continually inspired in my work by Debby Hirshman of the JCC of Manhattan, whose unique ability to bring people together and then allow their own agendas and passions to emerge convinced me that community and autonomy are not mutually exclusive, but interdependent.

I am also extremely grateful to the doorman of my building, Jerzy Prus, who also happens to be one of the world's leading historians (he won't let me credit him as an Egyptologist, though his hundreds of publications indicate otherwise). His knowledge of the customs and religions of ancient Egypt were very instrumental in helping me develop a more comprehensive understanding of the early Israelite period.

Thanks are also due to Zöe Baird, Julia Moffett, and, especially, my mentor Alice Cahn, of the Markle Foundation, whose generosity made the research phase of this book possible.

This book is also a reflection of many late-night discussions with friends who had to put up with me for the past two years of soul searching. Thanks especially to David Bennahum, Red Burns, Craig Kanarick, David Pescovitz, Bennett Rushkoff, Andrew Shapiro, Dan Sieradski, and everyone at Harmony Lodge for seeing me through this process.

A heartfelt thanks to Doug Pepper, my menschly über-editor, and everyone at Crown for supporting not only this book, but also what it is intended to do. I've never experienced a team effort quite on this scale before. I'm also deeply indebted to my agent, Jay Mandel, for finding me such a welcoming literary home, and Lisa Shotland, who has kept her eye on the big picture for a decade.

And finally, thanks to you, dear reader, for supporting my writing and for considering what I have to say. Without you, there would be no me.

INDEX

ABOUT THE AUTHOR

DOUGLAS RUSHKOFF is the author of eight critically acclaimed books that have been translated into more than fifteen languages. His radio commentaries air on National Public Radio's *All Things Considered,* and his monthly column on cyberculture, distributed through the New York Times Syndicate, appears in more than thirty countries. Rushkoff lectures about media, art, society, and religion at conferences and universities around the world. He hosts and writes documentaries for PBS, Channel Four, and the BBC and has won numerous awards, including the Marshall McLuhan Award for Outstanding Book in the Field of Media Ecology.

Visit the author's website at http://www.rushkoff.com.